ASVAB Armed Services Vocational Aptitude Battery Flashcards

By: Sharon A Wynne, M.S.

XAMonline, INC.
Boston

XAMonline, Inc.
21 Orient Avenue
Melrose, MA 02176
Toll Free 1-800-509-4128
Email: info@xamonline.com
Web: www.xamonline.com
Fax: 1-617-583-5552

Library of Congress Cataloging-in-Publication Data

Wynne, Sharon A.
   ASVAB Armed Services Vocational Aptitude Battery Flashcards / Sharon A. Wynne. – 3rd ed. ISBN 978-1-60787-487-4
   1. ASVAB   2. AFQT   3. Study Guide
   4. Military   5. Careers

Disclaimer:
The opinions expressed in this publication are the sole works of XAMonline and were created independently from the various branches of the United States military.

Between the time of publication and printing, test standards as well as testing formats and website information may change that is not included in part or in whole within this product. Sample test questions are developed by XAMonline and reflect similar content as on real tests; however, they are not former tests. XAMonline assembles content that aligns with test standards but makes no claims nor guarantees test candidates a passing score.

Printed in the United States of America   œ-1
ASVAB Armed Services Vocational Aptitude Battery Flashcards
ISBN: 978-1-60787-487-4

Cover photos by videodet/iStock/Thinkstock and fcknimages/iStock/Thinkstock

TABLE OF CONTENTS

The ASVAB (Armed Forces Vocational Aptitude Battery)

WHAT IS THE ASVAB?

The Armed Services Vocational Aptitude Battery (ASVAB) is an aptitude test developed by the Department of Defense. The ASVAB determines whether you are qualified to join the military and which civilian and military occupations might be a good fit for you.

The ASVAB assesses your strengths and weaknesses in a wide range of areas—from math and vocabulary to automotive maintenance and electrical circuits. It is a timed multiple-choice test made up of ten subtests, each covering a different subject area.

- Word Knowledge
- Paragraph Comprehension
- Arithmetic Reasoning
- Mathematics Knowledge
- General Science
- Mechanical Comprehension
- Electronics Information
- Shop Information*
- Auto Information*
- Assembling Objects

In the paper-and-pencil version the ASVAB, Shop Information and Auto Information are combined into one subtest.

Information about the ASVAB is subject to change, so please speak to a recruiter for the most up-to-date information on any aspect of the test.

What is an AFQT score? Why is it important?

Your Armed Forces Qualification Test (AFQT) score is critical if you have a desire to join the military. You must have a minimum qualifying score in order to enlist.

Your AFQT score is computed using four of the subtests:

- Word Knowledge
- Paragraph Comprehension
- Arithmetic Reasoning
- Mathematics Knowledge

AFQT scores are given as a percentage. If you score, for instance, a 65, it means that you scored as well as or better than 65% of a nationally representative group of people who took the test.

Different service branches require different AFQT scores. Contact your local recruiter to learn the current minimum qualifying scores.

Why is the ASVAB score important?

Composite scores from all of the subtests of the ASVAB help match new recruits to military occupations. Contact your local recruiter to learn which subtests are most important for specific military jobs.

VERSIONS OF THE ASVAB

There are two versions of the ASVAB used for military enlistment. The CAT-ASVAB, which is taken on a computer, and the Paper and Pencil ASVAB (P&P-ASVAB).

Both versions cover the same subjects. However, the Paper and Pencil ASVAB combines Shop Information and Auto Information into one subtest.

CAT-ASVAB

Today, most people who want to enlist in the military take the CAT-ASVAB. CAT is short for *computer adaptive testing*.

You must take the CAT-ASVAB at a Military Entrance Processing Station (MEPS). While you take the CAT-ASVAB on a computer, no computer experience is necessary. Everyone who takes the test receives training on any basic keyboard or mouse skills needed to take the test.

When you take the CAT-ASVAB, your answers are automatically recorded, your subtests are scored, and your AFQT score is computed. You will receive your scores as soon as you complete the test.

The CAT-ASVAB is made up of ten subtests.

Subtest	Questions	Minutes	Topics
Word Knowledge	16	8	Vocabulary knowledge, synonyms, and antonyms
Paragraph Comprehension	11	22	Reading comprehension, obtaining information from written passages
Arithmetic Reasoning	16	39	Solving word problems
Mathematics Knowledge	16	20	Mathematical concepts, algebra, and geometry
General Science	16	8	Biology, physics, chemistry, and earth and space science
Mechanical Comprehension	16	20	Principles of mechanics and mechanical devices
Electronics Information	16	8	Electrical current, circuits, and devices
Shop Information	11	6	Tools and wood and metal shop practices
Auto Information	11	7	Automotive knowledge, maintenance, and repair
Assembling Objects	16	16	Assembling parts into objects and connecting labeled parts
Total	145	154	

The CAT-ASVAB is an adaptive test, which means that the difficulty of the questions changes depending on how well you are doing. If you answer a question correctly, the next question will usually be more difficult. If you answer a question incorrectly, the next question will be easier. That way, you do not spend your time answering questions that are far too easy or hard for you. CAT-ASVAB scores are based not only on whether your answers are correct, but also on how difficult the questions are.

Unlike on the Paper and Pencil ASVAB, you cannot go back and change an answer on the CAT-ASVAB. However, the CAT-ASVAB allows you to go on to the next subtest if you finish a subtest early, and you can leave the room when you complete the entire test.

Paper and Pencil ASVAB

The Paper and Pencil ASVAB (P&P-ASVAB), which you may choose in lieu of the CAT-ASVAB, is a test that you take on paper at a Mobile Examination Test (MET) site. The P&P-ASVAB is made up of nine subtests.

Subtest	Questions	Minutes	Topics
Word Knowledge	35	11	Vocabulary knowledge, synonyms, and antonyms
Paragraph Comprehension	15	13	Reading comprehension, obtaining information from written passages
Arithmetic Reasoning	30	36	Solving word problems
Mathematics Knowledge	25	24	Mathematical concepts, algebra, and geometry
General Science	25	11	Biology, physics, chemistry, and earth and space science
Mechanical Comprehension	25	19	Principles of mechanics and mechanical devices
Electronics Information	20	9	Electrical current, circuits, and devices
Auto and Shop Information	25	11	Automotive knowledge, maintenance, and repair; tools and wood and metal shop practices
Assembling Objects	25	15	Assembling parts into objects and connecting labeled parts
Total	225	149	

When you take the P&P-ASVAB, you write your answers on an answer sheet. You have a certain amount of time to finish each subtest. Within that time, you can go back and change an answer. However, you cannot go back to a previous subtest. You also cannot begin the next subtest until the test administer instructs you to.

After you have taken the test, your P&P-ASVAB answer sheet is sent to the MEPS. Your recruiter will let you know when your scores are available. It usually takes a few days for your test to be scored.

ASVAB CAREER EXPLORATION PROGRAM FOR STUDENTS

High school and college students can take the ASVAB as part of the ASVAB Career Exploration Program. The ASVAB helps students learn more about which careers might be a good match for their knowledge, skills, and abilities.

Students who take advantage of this program take the Paper and Pencil ASVAB. The Assembling Objects subtest is not included in this version for students.

While this version of the ASVAB is used primarily for career exploration, you are in fact able to use your score to enlist in the military for up to two years.

1. *Word Knowledge*

What is a noun?

2. *Word Knowledge*

What is an adjective?

3. *Word Knowledge*

What is a verb?

1.

Noun (*n*): A noun is word used to indicate a person, place, thing or idea.

2.

Adjective (*adj*): An adjective describes or modifies a noun. It often appears in front of the noun it describes, such as "blue" in "blue eyes" or "twenty" in "twenty spectators" or "harmonious" in "harmonious relationships" but may appear in other parts of the sentence too.

3.

Verb (*v*): Verbs are words that express action, a state of being, or that link the subject of the sentence to further thoughts on the subject.

A sentence cannot be a sentence without a subject and a verb. "He is" is a full sentence because it has a subject ("He") and a verb ("is").

4.   *Word Knowledge*

What is an adverb?

5.   *Word Knowledge*

What is the definition of a synonym and an antonym?

6.   *Word Knowledge*

Abhorrence

4.

Adverb (*adv*): An adverb describes a verb; it tells how something was done, as in "he described the incident accurately" with "accurately" being the adverb, telling how he did something. An adverb also may describe an adjective or another adverb. For example, in the sentence "Her scintillatingly green eyes met his with impact," "scintillatingly" is an adverb describing the adjective "green" and modifying what kind of green her eyes were.

5.

Synonym: A word that is the same as or similar to another word in meaning.

Antonym: A word that is the opposite of another word in meaning.

6.

Definition: Abhorrence (*n*): a sense or feeling of hatred, disgust, and revulsion.

Example: Although they used to be friends, after Christine found out Trevor had stolen money from the treasury, she could only look at him with **abhorrence.**

Synonym: repugnance, loathing
Antonym: pleasure, admiration

7. *Word Knowledge*

Amorphousness

8. *Word Knowledge*

Analogy

9. *Word Knowledge*

Animosity

7. *Word Knowledge*

Definition: Amorphousness (*n*): shapelessness, being of vague outline, being without contours or form.

Example: Captain Ahab saw a huge mass of pale **amorphousness** in the sea and he knew instantly that it was the great white whale Moby Dick.

Synonym: cloudiness, formlessness
Antonym: sharpness, distinctness

---

8. *Word Knowledge*

Definition: Analogy (*n*): a parallel or similarity between two different things that resemble each other in some points.

Example: The riddle "Humpty Dumpty" has sometimes been seen as an **analogy** between an egg that splattered on the pavement and a ruler who fell from power and came to ruin.

Synonym: comparison
Antonym: polarity, opposite

---

9. *Word Knowledge*

Definition: Animosity (*n*): hostility, anger, ill will.

Example: Tom felt no **animosity** toward Bill even though Bill was chosen over him to become captain of the team.

Synonym: resentment, grudge
Antonym: friendliness, affection

10.   *Word Knowledge*

Beneficence

11.   *Word Knowledge*

Bombast

12.   *Word Knowledge*

Catharsis

10.

Definition: Beneficence (*n*): a state or condition of being kind and doing good acts.

Example: Because of the king's **beneficence**, the poor were given free food on holidays.

Synonym: generosity, kindness
Antonym: cruelty, selfishness

11.

Definition: Bombast (*n*): pretentious, overblown, exaggerated speaking or writing.

Example: Edward Everett's lengthy speech at Gettysburg was long and full of dramatic parallels—some might say it was full of **bombast**—but Everett recognized that President Lincoln said more in two minutes than he had said in two hours.

Synonym: pomposity, "hot air"
Antonym: succinctness

12.

Definition: Catharsis (*n*): a mental and emotional climax and release; an event that lets out pent-up feelings and brings relief and peace.

Example: I finally spoke to my professor about how far behind I had fallen in her class, and her helpfulness and good advice gave me a sense of **catharsis.**

Synonym: purification
Antonym: tension

13. *Word Knowledge*

Chaos

14. *Word Knowledge*

Credibility

15. *Word Knowledge*

Dilemma

13.

Definition: Chaos (*n*): an unorganized, messy, disharmonious state of being.

Example: After the earthquake and tsunami, parts of Japan were in utter **chaos**, with displaced people, floating cars, ruined houses, and debris everywhere.

Synonym: pandemonium, mess
Antonym: orderliness

14.

Definition: Credibility (*n*): the quality of being believable and trustworthy.

Example: After he performed life-saving CPR on an employee who was having a heart attack, the new safety manager gained much **credibility** among the workers.

Synonym: believability, trustworthiness
Antonym: suspicion, mistrust

15.

Definition: Dilemma (*n*): a situation where a person is faced with difficult choices, none of which seem better than the other, and each of which may have negative consequences.

Example: I faced a painful **dilemma**: disobey my parents and go to the beach to stay with friends or upset my friends by refusing to go.

Synonym: conundrum, "pickle"
Antonym: solution, resolution

16. *Word Knowledge*

Disaffection

17. *Word Knowledge*

Discretion

18. *Word Knowledge*

Efficacy

16.

Definition: Disaffection (*n*): a state of being unhappy, discontented, and/or alienated.

Example: After two broken engagements, Charles went through several months of **disaffection** toward the opposite sex.

Synonym: disillusionment
Antonym: contentment, satisfaction

17.

Definition: Discretion (*n*): the ability to use good judgment and exercise consideration for others' feelings and needs.

Example: "I am counting on your **discretion**," the lawyer told his secretary when she had accidentally overhead a conversation protected by attorney-client privilege.

Synonym: sensibleness, sensitivity
Antonym: inconsideration, insensitivity

18.

Definition: Efficacy (*n*): ability to bring about a desire effect or outcome.

Example: I was not convinced of the **efficacy** of the communications technique until I tried it with my father and we understood each other better than ever before.

Synonym: effectiveness, success
Antonym: ineffectiveness, failure

19. *Word Knowledge*

Elocution

20. *Word Knowledge*

Gratuity

21. *Word Knowledge*

Happenstance

Definition: Elocution (*n*): proper pronunciation, voice projection, and the sum total of speaking well, especially publically.

Example: Because of a tendency to swallow his words, the would-be Hollywood actor took some **elocution** lessons.

Synonym: speaking, public speaking
Antonym: murmur, mumbling

Definition: Gratuity (*n*): something given for free, in addition, as in a monetary tip.

Example: Because the waiter gave them such exceptional service, the group decided to leave a generous **gratuity**.

Synonym: tip, favor
Antonym: wages, salary

Definition: Happenstance (*n*): an event that occurs by chance, simply as it happens.

Example: Sue met her husband by **happenstance**; they both tried to get into the same taxicab in New York City during a rain storm.

Synonym: serendipity, chance
Antonym: plan, scheme

22.   *Word Knowledge*

Integrity

---

23.   *Word Knowledge*

Itinerary

---

24.   *Word Knowledge*

Jurisdiction

22.

Definition: Integrity (*n*): a state of being whole, uncorrupted, sound.

Example: Because she refused to compromise her moral principles, Lorraine was known as a person of **integrity**.

Synonym: incorruptibility
Antonym: corruptibility, compromise

23.

Definition: Itinerary (*n*): a planned list of places to travel to.

Example: Intrigued by the country roads winding through French wine country, we ignored our **itinerary** of tourist spots and rented some bicycles for some impromptu explorations.

Synonym: route, tour, plan
Antonym: serendipity, happenstance

24.

Definition: Jurisdiction (*n*): an area in which one is responsible and has authority.

Example: "That's outside my **jurisdiction**," the father told his twenty-one-year-old son, "It's your decision now where you want to live."

Synonym: power, authority
Antonym: disempowerment

25. *Word Knowledge*

Machinations

26. *Word Knowledge*

Malfeasance

27. *Word Knowledge*

Miasma

25.

Definition: Machinations (*n*): crafty designs or schemes.

Example: My cousin met her husband through the **machinations** of my aunt: Aunt Clara invited the young man to a scrumptious dessert and then presented her daughter.

Synonym: maneuverings, manipulations
Antonym: guilelessness, happenstance

26.

Definition: Malfeasance (*n*): an act of corruption or dishonesty, often by someone in a public or responsible position.

Example: The fact that the mayor used the funds for the concrete road barrier to line his own in-ground swimming pool was considered an act of **malfeasance**.

Synonym: crime, wrongdoing
Antonym: charity, responsibility

27.

Definition: Miasma (*n*): an indistinct, foggy, smothering atmosphere.

Example: Because I could not make a decision, I wandered through my days in a **miasma** of uncertainty.

Synonym: obscurity, fog
Antonym: clarity

28.   *Word Knowledge*

Oxymoron

29.   *Word Knowledge*

Paradox

30.   *Word Knowledge*

Perseverance

28. *Word Knowledge*

Definition: Oxymoron (*n*): a contradiction in terms; words that contradict each other.

Example: Shakespeare's character said, "I must be cruel to be kind," and a "cruel kindness" is an **oxymoron**.

Synonym: contradiction
Antonym: parallel; similarity

---

29. *Word Knowledge*

Definition: Paradox (*n*): something that seems contradictory or nonsensical yet may be the true situation.

Example: It was a **paradox** that Bruce was more tired and irritable after he had spent all day watching television than Tim was after he had worked all day as a volunteer at the homeless shelter.

Synonym: irony
Antonym: sensible, reasonable

---

30. *Word Knowledge*

Definition: Perseverance (*n*): the quality of continuing on over time and in spite of adversity; not giving up.

Example: Olympic gold medalists are no doubt talented at what they do, but the **perseverance** to practice many hours a day, every day, for years on end, is indispensable to victory.

Synonym: persistence
Antonym: inconsistency

31.   *Word Knowledge*

Provocateur

32.   *Word Knowledge*

Prudence

33.   *Word Knowledge*

Remnant

31. *Word Knowledge*

Definition: Provocateur (*n*): the person or party in a quarrel who provokes the argument.

Example: Johnny kicked in Stevie's sand castle, and we know that Johnny has been the **provocateur** in many sandbox fights.

Synonym: provoker, agitator
Antonym: peacemaker

---

32. *Word Knowledge*

Definition: Prudence (*n*): the quality of having good, sound judgment; being sensible and wise.

Example: President Lincoln exercised great **prudence** in making sure the crucial border states in the Civil War remained in the Union, even though he had to make temporary compromises to keep them there.

Synonym: wisdom, judgment
Antonym: folly, foolishness

---

33. *Word Knowledge*

Definition: Remnant (*n*): small remaining pieces, a few left out of many or out of a former whole.

Example: By the time we left, only a **remnant** of the huge audience was still in the stadium.

Synonym: scraps, remains
Antonym: whole

34.

Word Knowledge

Scruples

35.

Word Knowledge

Stasis

36.

Word Knowledge

Tenet

34.

Definition: Scruples (*n*): moral principles; ethics; conscience.

Example: Joy, who was a meticulous bookkeeper, felt compelled by her **scruples** to become a whistleblower when she saw the firm's accountants "cooking the books."

Synonym: beliefs, morality
Antonym: immorality, amorality

35.

Definition: Stasis (*n*): a state of no movement; being stationary; being in balance; not flowing or circulating.

Example: The population of the earth seems to consistently arrive at **stasis** as far as the ratio of males to females: there is almost a one-to-one correspondence.

Synonym: stability; equilibrium
Antonym: flow, circulation

36.

Definition: Tenet (*n*): a belief; a fundamental principle.

Example: It is a **tenet** in our society that hard work will bring a person success.

Synonym: precept, teaching
Antonym: deviation, heresy

37. *Word Knowledge*

Tremulousness

38. *Word Knowledge*

Umbrage

39. *Word Knowledge*

Verities

37. *Word Knowledge*

Definition: Tremulousness (*n*): a state of trembling, uncertainty.

Example: She was a very famous celebrity, yet her **tremulousness** on the red carpet showed how shy she really was.

Synonym: timidity, insecurity
Antonym: confidence, firmness

38. *Word Knowledge*

Definition: Umbrage (*n*): a feeling of being offended or insulted.

Example: The teacher took **umbrage** when the student derided the book he had written.

Synonym: offense, resentment
Antonym: pride, flattery

39. *Word Knowledge*

Definition: Verities (*n*): assertions that stand the test of time; things that are true and hold true beyond time and place; first principles.

Example: The professor said that there were certain **verities,** like honesty in business dealings and courage in battle that have been valued and admired in all cultures throughout history.

Synonym: truths, principles
Antonym: lies, deceits

40. *Word Knowledge*

Vicissitudes

41. *Word Knowledge*

Wistfulness

42. *Word Knowledge*

Acrimonious

40.

Definition: Vicissitudes (*n*): ups and downs, twists and turns, unforeseen events, both good and bad.

Example: Marriage involves being able to adapt to the **vicissitudes** of life together.

Synonym: changes, fluctuations
Antonym: steadiness, routine

41.

Definition: Wistfulness (*n*): a wishful quality of missing or wanting something.

Example: When she described the mountains and valleys of her native land, her voice was full of **wistfulness.**

Synonym: yearning, longing
Antonym: rejection, denial

42.

Definition: Acrimonious (*adj*): discordant, bitter, quarrelsome.

Example: The family's relationships were **acrimonious** until each member learned to moderate his or her criticism of the others.

Synonym: sarcastic, biting
Antonym: sweet, harmonious

43.   *Word Knowledge*

Ardent

44.   *Word Knowledge*

Bellicose

45.   *Word Knowledge*

Benighted

43.

Definition: Ardent (*adj*): full of ardor, warmly attached or supportive, on fire for something.

Example: An animal lover ever since she was a little girl, Patricia was an **ardent** supporter of the local pet shelter.

Synonym: passionate
Antonym: indifferent

44.

Definition: Bellicose (*adj*): wanting to fight; wanting war.

Example: Although Jeff had nothing against Tom, Tom's **bellicose** attitude made it impossible not to argue with him occasionally.

Synonym: war-like, quarrelsome
Antonym: pacific, conciliatory

45.

Definition: Benighted (*adj*): troubled, beset with difficulties, full of darkness in a figurative sense.

Example: In Pearl S. Buck's famous novel *The Good Earth*, famine left parts of early twentieth century rural China **benighted**.

Synonym: stricken, disfavored
Antonym: enlightened, favored

46. *Word Knowledge*

Blighted

47. *Word Knowledge*

Capacious

48. *Word Knowledge*

Cursory

46.

Definition: Blighted (*adj*): affected by disease or disintegration; hindered or frustrated.

Example: Because he refused to work hard and take initiative, his hopes of attaining highly rewarding employment were **blighted**.

Synonym: spoiled
Antonym: robust, fulfilled

47.

Definition: Capacious (*adj*): of a large capacity; roomy; full of space.

Example: Because the village homes were built on former farmland, the lawns were **capacious,** with small natural streams and large trees.

Synonym: spacious
Antonym: cramped, crowded

48.

Definition: Cursory (*adj*): something that is done in a hurry and in a possibly shallow or careless way.

Example: She only did a **cursory** review of her notes before the exam, and she got a poor grade because of it.

Synonym: hurried, superficial
Antonym: detailed, painstaking

49.   *Word Knowledge*

Definitive

50.   *Word Knowledge*

Dissident

51.   *Word Knowledge*

Effervescent

49.

Definition: Definitive (*adj*): serving as the standard, even the "gold standard"; the perfect example; the final word.

Example: Marlon Brando's performance as Terry Malloy in the movie *On the Waterfront* is considered the **definitive** demonstration of method acting, a technique of using one's own life experiences to identify with the character one is portraying.

Synonym: conclusive, ultimate
Antonym: approximate

50.

Definition: Dissident (*adj*): to be in objection to, to be in protest against, to disagree with a given organization, system, or decision.

Example: The municipal board had a hard time keeping **dissident** members in order when it was revealed that a controversial traffic circle in the downtown area had increased motor vehicle accidents.

Synonym: protesting, disagreeing
Antonym: supportive

51.

Definition: Effervescent (*adj*): bubbling; bubbling over; sparkling.

Example: Many at the party felt drawn to Suzanne's **effervescent** personality as she laughed good-naturedly at people's jokes and made her own witty replies.

Synonym: vivacious, sprightly
Antonym: lifeless, dull

52. *Word Knowledge*

Ephemeral

53. *Word Knowledge*

Evocative

54. *Word Knowledge*

Excessive

52. *Word Knowledge*

Definition: Ephemeral (*adj*): passing quickly, fleeting, only there for a moment or a short time.

Example: As they watched the autumn sunset from their canoe on the lake, the group of friends sighed over the **ephemeral** joys of summer.

Synonym: short-lived, temporary
Antonym: durable, lasting

---

53. *Word Knowledge*

Definition: Evocative (*adj*): pulling out or calling forth certain emotions, thoughts or memories.

Example: Hearing the national anthem is an **evocative** moment for many people.

Synonym: emotional, affecting
Antonym: numbing, unfeeling

---

54. *Word Knowledge*

Definition: Excessive (*adj*): too much, overdone.

Example: When he saw his friend drinking **excessive** amounts of alcohol, Daniel said, "I'll drive."

Synonym: overmuch, unlimited
Antonym: limited, sparse

55. *Word Knowledge*

Expedient

56. *Word Knowledge*

Fastidious

57. *Word Knowledge*

Finite

55.

Definition: Expedient (*adj*): that which is convenient and effective in the short run or for a limited purpose.

Example: In his speech at the business conference, Harry said the company could not just take **expedient** measures to reduce its wastefulness.

Synonym: short-term, convenient
Antonym: far-seeing, visionary

56.

Definition: Fastidious (*adj*): very careful, neat, clean and exact; of high standards.

Example: The breath-taking beauty of the garden and grounds showed the gardener's **fastidious** care.

Synonym: meticulous
Antonym: sloppy, careless

57.

Definition: Finite (*adj*): extending or going only so far; limited in range or scope; unable to be replenished or renewed.

Example: Many natural resources are **finite** and need to be conserved in order to last.

Synonym: limited
Antonym: unlimited, infinite

58.
Word Knowledge

Impecunious

59.
Word Knowledge

Impermeable

60.
Word Knowledge

Incorporeal

58.

Definition: Impecunious (*adj*): without means, funds or money.

Example: Because he disliked working, the young man was **impecunious** and had to borrow from friends whenever they went out together to restaurants.

Synonym: broke, penniless
Antonym: rich, flush

59.

Definition: Impermeable (*adj*): unable to be penetrated; solid; not porous.

Example: The oilcloth slicker, although not fashionable, was an **impermeable** shield from the driving rain.

Synonym: impenetrable
Antonym: porous

60.

Definition: Incorporeal (*adj*): without a body; without physical, substantial form.

Example: Patriotism, honor, and selflessness are **incorporeal** qualities, yet they move people to do deeds that change the world.

Synonym: intangible, invisible
Antonym: bodily, earthly

61.
Word Knowledge

Inevitable

62.
Word Knowledge

Insidious

63.
Word Knowledge

Intractable

61. *Word Knowledge*

Definition: Inevitable (*adj*): had to happen; could not be prevented; completely to be expected.

Example: Even though we know the Titanic's **inevitable** fate, we hope our favorite characters will escape death as we watch the fictionalized movie.

Synonym: unavoidable, inexorable
Antonym: preventable, alterable

---

62. *Word Knowledge*

Definition: Insidious (*adj*): having a creeping, unnoticed, barely perceptible ill effect.

Example: Long term stress has an **insidious** affect on a person's health and wellbeing.

Synonym: subtle
Antonym: blatant

---

63. *Word Knowledge*

Definition: Intractable (*adj*): difficult to control or change; stubborn; refusing to be dislodged.

Example: The book *Death Be Not Proud* is about a young man's struggle with a brain tumor so **intractable** the surgeon can only remove part of it.

Synonym: unyielding, uncooperative
Antonym: pliant, yielding

64. *Word Knowledge*

Irrevocable

65. *Word Knowledge*

Malevolent

66. *Word Knowledge*

Mundane

64.

Definition: Irrevocable (*adj*): that something cannot be called back, taken back, or revoked.

Example: In Jane Austen's novel *Pride and Prejudice*, Elizabeth Bennett's refusal of Mr. Darcy's marriage proposal is **irrevocable** until he proves himself to be quite different than he appears to be.

Synonym: unchangeable
Antonym: flexible

65.

Definition: Malevolent (*adj*): evil; wanting to do harm.

Example: I thought the person tailgating me on the dark road had **malevolent** intentions, and so I drove straight to the brightly lit convenience store once I got into town.

Synonym: evil, ill-intentioned
Antonym: kindly, charitable

66.

Definition: Mundane (*adj*): ordinary; every day; routine.

Example: Nathaniel Hawthorne's wife saved up money and attended to the **mundane** aspects of their lives so that he could write his most famous work, *The Scarlett Letter*.

Synonym: commonplace
Antonym: extraordinary

67. *Word Knowledge*

Opaque

68. *Word Knowledge*

Perennial

69. *Word Knowledge*

Piquant

67. *Word Knowledge*

Definition: Opaque (*adj*): difficult to see through; blocked; not transparent (used literally to describe surfaces and figuratively to describe personalities or communications).

Example: Text messaging is an **opaque** form of communication because you cannot tell what the other person is really thinking.

Synonym: impermeable
Antonym: transparent

68. *Word Knowledge*

Definition: Perennial (*adj*): coming back again and again; blooming once more; everlasting.

Example: Her **perennial** optimism both cheers and annoys me!

Synonym: never-ending
Antonym: temporary; impermanent

69. *Word Knowledge*

Definition: Piquant (*adj*): stimulating; tasty; enticingly delicious (may be used literally or figuratively).

Example: The **piquant** spices in the cooking stew made Larry badger his mother as to when it would be ready to eat.

Synonym: mouth-watering
Antonym: tasteless; flat

70.   *Word Knowledge*

Porous

71.   *Word Knowledge*

Pseudo

72.   *Word Knowledge*

Recalcitrant

70.

Definition: Porous (*adj*): permeable; with spaces or holes large enough to absorb liquid; to allow passage through.

Example: The **porous** border between the two countries was a smuggler's paradise.

Synonym: penetrable, permeable
Antonym: impenetrable, impermeable

71.

Definition: Pseudo (*adj*): semi-; not completely; halfway; so-called.

Example: She considers him a **pseudo**-intellectual—he is not as well-informed as he pretends.

Synonym: quasi; phony
Antonym: authentic, thoroughgoing

72.

Definition: Recalcitrant (*adj*): stubbornly defiant; willfully disobedient and badly behaved.

Example: "You're acting like a **recalcitrant** schoolboy by refusing to dress according to school standards," the principal told the defiant young teacher.

Synonym: intractable; resistant
Antonym: compliant, docile

73. *Word Knowledge*

Reverberating

74. *Word Knowledge*

Scintillating

75. *Word Knowledge*

Sequestered

73.

Definition: Reverberating (*adj*): vibrating or echoing; repeating.

Example: The **reverberating** cymbals added to the climactic drama of the symphony.

Synonym: percussive
Antonym: silence

74.

Definition: Scintillating (*adj*): sparkling, witty, brilliant.

Example: "Even after it went out, the bonfire was more **scintillating** than the conversation at that party," Alan complained to Alexandra.

Synonym: bright, stimulating
Antonym: dull, dreary

75.

Definition: Sequestered (*adj*): isolated; kept from interaction; protected.

Example: The **sequestered** jury in the play *Twelve Angry Men* gets into many arguments as they consider the death penalty for a defendant and question one another's motivations.

Synonym: secluded
Antonym: desegregated

76. *Word Knowledge*

Specious

77. *Word Knowledge*

Tenacious

78. *Word Knowledge*

Translucent

76. *Word Knowledge*

Definition: Specious (*adj*): false but seemingly genuine; impressive without substance; fancily deceptive.

Example: Although the company had a well-designed website which showcased their impressive clients, further investigation showed their claims were **specious**, as few of those well-known people had ever used the company's services.

Synonym: deceitful, bombastic
Antonym: sound, logical

---

77. *Word Knowledge*

Definition: Tenacious (*adj*): not easily letting go; persistent; holding to something.

Example: Had it not been for the boss's **tenacious** refusal to give up, the firm would have declared bankruptcy two years ago.

Synonym: stubborn, unrelenting
Antonym: weak, yielding

---

78. *Word Knowledge*

Definition: Translucent (*adj*): allowing some light to filter through; sheer or see-through.

Example: The newborn baby's **translucent** skin allowed blue veins to be seen clearly at his temples.

Synonym: diaphanous
Antonym: opaque

79. *Word Knowledge*

Transcendent

80. *Word Knowledge*

Abjure

81. *Word Knowledge*

Admonished

79.

Definition: Transcendent: (*adj*): going beyond and above; rising above the usual, mundane or earthly.

Example: When we experienced our second wind and ran to the crest of the mountain, the view of the earth and clouds was a **transcendent** experience and we were ecstatic.

Synonym: spiritual, metaphysical
Antonym: worldly, fleshly

80.

Definition: Abjure (*v*): to swear off, to proclaim a formal or official rejection.

Example: Sir Thomas More refused to sign an oath supporting King Henry the 8th's absolute authority and second marriage (Henry would marry four more times), saying he could not **abjure** his conscience.

Synonym: repudiate, deny
Antonym: endorse

81.

Definition: Admonished (*v*): warned; advised in order to help someone; reminded.

Example: The mother continually **admonished** her teenage sons to wear seatbelts, saying seatbelts lowered fatalities in car accidents by 50%.

Synonym: scolded
Antonym: allowed

82. *Word Knowledge*

Affirm

83. *Word Knowledge*

Aspire

84. *Word Knowledge*

Bestow

82. *Word Knowledge*

Definition: Affirm (*v*): to agree with something; to support something or someone with positive assertions.

Example: The employer took the phone call from the bank to **affirm** that her employee made a salary sufficient to sustain the repayment of a proposed bank loan.

Synonym: reinforce, verify
Antonym: invalidate

---

83. *Word Knowledge*

Definition: Aspire (*v*): to hope for something; to dream of something; to wish and want to attain some state of being or achievement.

Example: The TV show *American Idol* showcases people who **aspire** to musical fame.

Synonym: envision
Antonym: surrender

---

84. *Word Knowledge*

Definition: Bestow (*v*): to give, to give time, attention or a gift.

Example: "How kind of you to **bestow** your company upon us!" the hostess said to the visiting dignitary.

Synonym: donate, devote
Antonym: retain, revoke

85. *Word Knowledge*

Calcify

86. *Word Knowledge*

Calumniate

87. *Word Knowledge*

Codify

85.

Definition: Calcify (*v*): to harden, to make brittle.

Example: "At lot of people let their ideas **calcify** as they age, but the minds of the young are flexible," said the visiting lecturer.

Synonym: solidify
Antonym: flex, bend

86.

Definition: Calumniate (*v*): to say bad things about another; to attempt to ruin someone's reputation by malicious words.

Example: "I don't appreciate your efforts to **calumniate** my family," I told my neighbor, who had been gossiping about me door to door ever since we'd had an argument about the boundaries of our properties.

Synonym: slander
Antonym: praise

87.

Definition: Codify (*v*): to code; to systematize; to put something into recognizable categories and regulations.

Example: The teacher decided to **codify** her many rules, but she found one maxim that said it all: "Treat others the way you would like to be treated."

Synonym: analyze, organize
Antonym: scramble

88. *Word Knowledge*

Conflate

89. *Word Knowledge*

Devise

90. *Word Knowledge*

Edify

88.

Definition: Conflate (*v*): to bring together; to blend, to equate.

Example: "Don't **conflate** optimism with blindness to reality—they are not the same thing," Melissa admonished her cynical friend Sam.

Synonym: combine, synthesize
Antonym: separate

89.

Definition: Devise (*v*): to construct in one's mind; to create a plan; to engage in original thinking.

Example: What I liked about Henry was his ability to **devise** strategies for solving problems no one else could even imagine.

Synonym: strategize
Antonym: deconstruct, copy

90.

Definition: Edify (*v*): to build up, to make stronger or better, to lift up with wisdom and good instruction.

Example: That movie did not **edify** me; in fact, it left me feeling depressed and hopeless.

Synonym: improve, support
Antonym: distress, destroy

91.

Word Knowledge

Emancipate

92.

Word Knowledge

Equivocate

93.

Word Knowledge

Erode

91.

Definition: Emancipate: (*v*): to set at liberty; set free, to lift previous constraints upon people.

Example: To **emancipate** a people from oppression must be a heady and joyous feeling.

Synonym: liberate
Antonym: imprison, enslave

92.

Definition: Equivocate (*v*): to use deceptive language; to go back and forth about something in an attempt to disguise the truth.

Example: Blair tried to **equivocate** as to why he had never called Blanche: "I was sick; I was busy; I was busy being sick!" he said.

Synonym: lie, deceive
Antonym: affirm, reveal

93.

Definition: Erode (*v*): to eat away; to wear away; to have decay set in and slowly destroy.

Example: The net effect of the many hidden fees involved in maintaining the savings account was to **erode** any savings.

Synonym: decay, corrode
Antonym: strengthen, edify

94.   *Word Knowledge*

Exhort

95.   *Word Knowledge*

Explicate

96.   *Word Knowledge*

Expurgate

94.

Definition: Exhort (*v*): to call to action by impassioned speech; to urge and excite.

Example: Alicia's father told her he did not mean to lecture her, but he did want to **exhort** her to quit smoking.

Synonym: incite
Antonym: calm, quell

95.

Definition: Explicate: (*v*): to explain logically, to lay out all the points, to elaborate upon in a detailed manner.

Example: The insurance form required me to **explicate**, in detail, exactly what happened on the day of the accident.

Synonym: elucidate, analyze
Antonym: hint, allude

96.

Definition: Expurgate (*v*): to cut out compromising or embarrassing or morally questionable material.

Example: The writers' circle asked the new member to **expurgate** his works before presenting them in a mixed setting of men and women and young and old.

Synonym: expunge, purify
Antonym: eroticize, sensualize

97. *Word Knowledge*

Grapple

98. *Word Knowledge*

Impart

99. *Word Knowledge*

Meander

97.

Definition: Grapple (*v*): to wrestle with; to grasp or grip; to come to terms or come to grips with.

Example: The *On the Waterfront* character Terry Malloy had to **grapple** with his loyalty to the mob and their increasing violence, injustice, and mistreatment of people.

Synonym: strive, contend
Antonym: submit

98.

Definition: Impart (*v*): to give; to pass down; to bequeath, especially knowledge and understanding, or to "give part of" a quantity of something.

Example: Most parents desire nothing more than to **impart** their wisdom, values, and understanding of life to their children.

Synonym: bestow, bequeath
Antonym: take, withhold

99.

Definition: Meander (*v*): to wander casually without direction; to walk or make a winding path.

Example: The quiet Sunday afternoon was a perfect time to **meander** through the forest preserve, drinking in sunshine and birdsong.

Synonym: saunter, stroll
Antonym: march, run

100. *Word Knowledge*

Obfuscate

101. *Word Knowledge*

Personify

102. *Word Knowledge*

Prevaricate

100. *Word Knowledge*

Definition: Obfuscate: (*v*) to make less clear; to make dim; to confuse or disguise.

Example: "Stop trying to confuse the jury!" the prosecutor said to the witness. "You are trying to **obfuscate** what really happened the night of the murder!"

Synonym: obscure
Antonym: clarify

---

101. *Word Knowledge*

Definition: Personify (*v*): to embody or to serve as the human or human-like example of abstract qualities.

Example: To the athletes, the coach was able to **personify** all the things he tried to teach them: he always set the example of fair play, honor, and determination.

Synonym: exemplify
Antonym: idealize

---

102. *Word Knowledge*

Definition: Prevaricate (*v*): to lie; to present conflicting information in order to deceive.

Example: "Don't **prevaricate**," said the boss to the worker, "it was not because of the holiday these papers were delayed as they were due long before the holiday."

Synonym: equivocate
Antonym: admit, confess

103. *Word Knowledge*

Propitiate

104. *Word Knowledge*

Proscribe

105. *Word Knowledge*

Protrude

103.

Definition: Propitiate (*v*): to blot out a bad record with someone; to mollify someone or make up for one's mistakes.

Example: To **propitiate** her wrongs against the investors in her phony scheme, the repentant defrauder sought to pay them back with the money from her inheritance.

Synonym: indemnify, compensate
Antonym: irritate, aggravate

104.

Definition: Proscribe (*v*): to forbid; to prevent an activity by naming it wrong or harmful.

Example: The Amish **proscribe** car ownership because they fear mobility will cause families and community members to spend too much time away from one another and grow apart.

Synonym: prohibit
Antonym: allow, permit

105.

Definition: Protrude (*v*): to stick out, to stand out, to project outward.

Example: If Cyrano de Bergerac's nose didn't **protrude** so much, he might have won his lady's favor instead of being a tragic poet whose beauty was hidden inside him.

Synonym: extend, jut
Antonym: shrink, hide

106. *Word Knowledge*

Recapitulate

107. *Word Knowledge*

Relinquish

108. *Word Knowledge*

Revivify

106. *Word Knowledge*

Definition: Recapitulate (*v*): to restate the major points of something; to recount events by the main points.

Example: "Please **recapitulate** what happened the afternoon you slipped on the ice," the doctor said. "It will help me to pinpoint your injuries."

Synonym: summarize
Antonym: detail

---

107. *Word Knowledge*

Definition: Relinquish (*v*): to let go of, to release, to give up.

Example: We asked the people who had been there a long time to **relinquish** leadership of the committee so that some newcomers could bring in fresh ideas.

Synonym: surrender, yield
Antonym: retain

---

108. *Word Knowledge*

Definition: Revivify (*v*): to bring back to life; to inject new life into something.

Example: Don't **revivify** that old argument; I thought we settled that long ago.

Synonym: resuscitate, revitalize
Antonym: decline, decay

109.

Revoke

110.

Soliloquize

111.

Stanch

WORD KNOWLEDGE

109. *Word Knowledge*

Definition: Revoke (*v*): to call back, to recall, to take away.

Example: If you do not pass the vision test, the Department of Motor Vehicles will **revoke** your driving privileges.

Synonym: recall, cancel
Antonym: bestow, endow

---

110. *Word Knowledge*

Definition: Soliloquize (*v*): to talk alone or to talk to oneself as in a reflection; to engage in a monologue.

Example: For hundreds of years audiences have enjoyed watching Hamlet **soliloquize** about action versus inaction and "to be or not to be."

Synonym: reflect
Antonym: converse, interact

---

111. *Word Knowledge*

Definition: Stanch (*v*): to stop the flow of; to prevent from spreading.

Example: Once he lanced the huge boil, the doctor used a cloth to **stanch** the flow of the infected pus.

Synonym: plug, check
Antonym: loosen, unplug

112. *Word Knowledge*

Sustain

113. *Word Knowledge*

Temper

114. *Word Knowledge*

Transmute

112. *Word Knowledge*

Definition: Sustain (*v*): to keep going; to support in an ongoing way; to hold up.

Example: The bridge could not **sustain** the pressure of the flood waters and it collapsed.

Synonym: bear
Antonym: break, collapse

---

113. *Word Knowledge*

Definition: Temper (*v*): to alter the effects of something; to season; to mix.

Example: Shakespeare's Portia advised that Shylock should **temper** strict justice with kindly mercy.

Synonym: soften, adjust
Antonym: insist

---

114. *Word Knowledge*

Definition: Transmute (*v*): to change into a better or more perfect state or being or form or appearance.

Example: "I want you to **transmute** your foolhardiness into courage—that is take risks for a purpose rather than just to be a daredevil," the coach told the young athlete.

Synonym: transform
Antonym: stabilize

115. *Word Knowledge*

Traverse

116. *Word Knowledge*

Trivialize

117. *Word Knowledge*

Verify

115. *Word Knowledge*

Definition: Traverse (*v*): to go across, to travel across, to move along or extend over.

Example: In *The Lord of the Rings*, the hobbits **traverse** many miles and much terrain to destroy the corrupting Ring of Power in the fiery Cracks of Doom.

Synonym: travel, cross
Antonym: stay, immobilize

---

116. *Word Knowledge*

Definition: Trivialize (*v*): to make small or to make into a small matter; to try to make something unimportant.

Example: "When you tell me to just take some over the counter medicine, I feel you are trying to **trivialize** how sick I really am," Clara said to her friend Susan.

Synonym: discount, minimize
Antonym: exaggerate

---

117. *Word Knowledge*

Definition: Verify (*v*): to validate; to make certain something is true.

Example: "Just let me **verify** your shipping address—do you still live at 147 Robin Road in Hillsdale, Missouri?" asked the person taking the order over the phone.

Synonym: confirm
Antonym: deny

118. *Word Knowledge*

Adamantly

119. *Word Knowledge*

Aptly

120. *Word Knowledge*

Assiduously

118. *Word Knowledge*

Definition: Adamantly (*adv*): dogmatically; with great emphasis or strength; brooking no other opinion or argument.

Example: He expressed himself so **adamantly**, no one at the table dared to argue with him.

Synonym: firmly, strongly
Antonym: doubtfully, questioningly

---

119. *Word Knowledge*

Definition: Aptly (*adv*): appropriately; with talent and accuracy; fittingly.

Example: I really did not think Jonas was going to be a good class president, but I was amazed at how **aptly** he fulfilled his duties.

Synonym: deftly
Antonym: clumsily, inappropriately

---

120. *Word Knowledge*

Definition: Assiduously (*adv*): to do something with great care and diligence; to pay great attention to detail; actively.

Example: Americans **assiduously** began paying down household debt during the recent recession.

Synonym: diligently, meticulously
Antonym: carelessly, cursorily

121. *Word Knowledge*

Begrudgingly

122. *Word Knowledge*

Cataclysmically

123. *Word Knowledge*

Cogently

121. *Word Knowledge*

Definition: Begrudgingly (*adv*): to do something while holding a grudge about it; inwardly unhappy about having to do or give something; giving something up with resentment.

Example: Trevor **begrudgingly** congratulated Allen on winning the MVP award, all the while thinking that he, Trevor, should have won it.

Synonym: resentfully, sullenly
Antonym: cheerfully, willingly

---

122. *Word Knowledge*

Definition: Cataclysmically (*adv*): something that occurs in an extraordinary, calamitous way; something that reaches the heights of controversy, destruction or change.

Example: Pearl Harbor **cataclysmically** impacted United States involvement in World War II.

Synonym: climactically
Antonym: calmly, regularly

---

123. *Word Knowledge*

Definition: Cogently: (*adv*): convincingly; with the power to persuade; honing in on clearly relevant points.

Example: Her ability to argue **cogently** about taxes and land use will help her be effective as the leader of the community drive to build an additional high school.

Synonym: relevantly, compellingly
Antonym: loosely, disjointedly

124. *Word Knowledge*

Condescendingly

125. *Word Knowledge*

Congenially

126. *Word Knowledge*

Covertly

124. *Word Knowledge*

Definition: Condescendingly (*adv*): acting or speaking in a manner that implies the speaker or actor is superior to the person being acted upon or spoken to; looking down on someone.

Example: Although the famous actress was obliging when I asked for her autograph, she acted so **condescendingly**, I never went to another one of her films.

Synonym: arrogantly, snobbishly
Antonym: humbly

125. *Word Knowledge*

Definition: Congenially (*adv*): getting along well together; agreeably; being well-suited to one another.

Example: I did not know if my father and father-in-law would get along, but I was pleased when I saw them conversing **congenially** over cocktails.

Synonym: harmoniously, compatibly
Antonym: argumentatively

126. *Word Knowledge*

Definition: Covertly (*adv*): in a covered way; in a way that is not out in the open, revealed, or admitted.

Example: In Dickens's book *Oliver Twist*, Mr. Bumble courts Mrs. Corney, all the while **covertly** checking the drawers in her home to see how much silver she owns.

Synonym: sneakily, unobtrusively
Antonym: openly

127. *Word Knowledge*

Credibly

128. *Word Knowledge*

Diligently

129. *Word Knowledge*

Disparagingly

127.

Definition: Credibly (*adv*): believably, in a way that inspires confidence and trust; having the background or credentials to be believed.

Example: If you have been cheating on your taxes, you cannot **credibly** claim to be a person of good character.

Synonym: validly
Antonym: unbelievably, incredibly

128.

Definition: Diligently (*adv*): to apply oneself with eagerness to work; to work or study hard; to be sincere about getting things done.

Example: The new worker set himself to his task so **diligently**, even the boss was impressed.

Synonym: earnestly, responsibly
Antonym: lazily, carelessly

129.

Definition: Disparagingly (*adv*): to speak in a way so as to put another person down; to run another person or thing down.

Example: Bella Swann in the *Twilight* series loved her beat-up and ancient Chevy truck, even if others looked **disparagingly** at the gas guzzler.

Synonym: slightingly, disrespectfully
Antonym: glowingly, respectfully

130. *Word Knowledge*

Eloquently

131. *Word Knowledge*

Empathically

132. *Word Knowledge*

Explicitly

130. *Word Knowledge*

Definition: Eloquently (*adv*): speaking smoothly and affectingly; having many apt words; speaking in a flow that moves people to listen and agree.

Example: Tyler was not much of a nature lover, but when he heard Miranda **eloquently** describe the wonders of mountain climbing, he began to think he was missing out on something.

Synonym: fluently, persuasively
Antonym: hesitantly, weakly

---

131. *Word Knowledge*

Definition: Empathically (*adv*): with empathy; able to identify with and relate to someone else's words, thoughts, or feelings; with sensitivity and understanding.

Example: All the girls loved to talk to Michael because he was able to listen so **empathically** to their concerns.

Synonym: sympathetically
Antonym: unsympathetically, uncaringly

---

132. *Word Knowledge*

Definition: Explicitly (*adv*): clearly; spelling something out so that it is clear; detailed; definite.

Example: "I **explicitly** told you the book report had to be on a fictional, not a non-fictional, work," the teacher told the student.

Synonym: indubitably, specifically
Antonym: vaguely, unclearly

133. *Word Knowledge*

Exquisitely

134. *Word Knowledge*

Extraneously

135. *Word Knowledge*

Glibly

133. *Word Knowledge*

Definition: Exquisitely (*adv*): done exceptionally beautifully in taste and design; extraordinarily well-rendered; extremely pleasing artistically or aesthetically.

Example: In the Vancouver Winter Olympics, Evgeni Pluschenko landed the difficult quadruple jump in an uneven performance, but Evan Lysacek performed so **exquisitely** throughout his entire robust program, he took home the gold without doing the spectacular jump.

Synonym: flawlessly, perfectly
Antonym: clumsily, imperfectly

---

134. *Word Knowledge*

Definition: Extraneously: (*adv*): coming from the outside; being outside of or beside the main point; not internally related to what is going on.

Example: It was difficult to hold a discussion with him because he kept bringing things up **extraneously** and taking the conversation off onto tangents.

Synonym: extrinsically, tangentially
Antonym: intrinsically, cogently

---

135. *Word Knowledge*

Definition: Glibly (*adv*): easily said; said without much thought; smoothly said but shallow.

Example: "You say you're going to become a biochemist so **glibly**," Tanya said to Danny, "but is it really going to be that easy?"

Synonym: superficially, sleekly
Antonym: profoundly

136. *Word Knowledge*

Implicitly

137. *Word Knowledge*

Inaudibly

138. *Word Knowledge*

Incongruously

136. *Word Knowledge*

Definition: Implicitly (*adv*): said by implication rather than outright; understood without words.

Example: Charles VII is sometimes depicted as **implicitly** giving Joan of Arc permission to try to wrest Paris from the English but not daring to give her enough support to ensure her victory.

Synonym: wordlessly
Antonym: outspokenly

137. *Word Knowledge*

Definition: Inaudibly (*adv*): so soft as to be unheard; something that cannot be heard by the human ear.

Example: The shy girl answered all of the interviewer's questions, but she answered them so **inaudibly** she did not get the job.

Synonym: softly, incomprehensively
Antonym: audibly, loudly

138. *Word Knowledge*

Definition: Incongruously (*adv*): inconsistently; not going together well; discordant elements mingled together.

Example: Among the sea of black umbrellas surrounding the government official who was commenting to reporters on the street, Seth's neon yellow umbrella stood out **incongruously**.

Synonym: inappropriately
Antonym: compatibly; harmoniously

139. *Word Knowledge*

Indubitably

140. *Word Knowledge*

Ineffably

141. *Word Knowledge*

Intrinsically

139.

Definition: Indubitably (*adv*): without a doubt; of a certainty; obviously.

Example: In Shakespeare's *Hamlet,* Polonious says that it follows **indubitably**, as the night follows the day, that being true to oneself is the best way not to be false to others.

Synonym: certainly, undoubtedly
Antonym: doubtfully, uncertainly

140.

Definition: Ineffably (*adv*): incapable of being expressed through words; indescribably; understood only by the heart or intuition.

Example: He was so **ineffably** happy to be with the woman he loved, he found himself walking in a daze and unable to stop grinning.

Synonym: wordlessly, inexpressibly
Antonym: vociferously, wordily

141.

Definition: Intrinsically (*adv*): coming from within; innately; arising from the original nature of something.

Example: The Declaration of Independence asserts that rights arise **intrinsically** as opposed to being bestowed by government.

Synonym: inalienable, intrinsic
Antonym: extrinsic, external

142. *Word Knowledge*

Irreparably

143. *Word Knowledge*

Lamentably

144. *Word Knowledge*

Laudably

142.

Definition: Irreparably: (*adv*): unable to be repaired; unable to be made whole again; breached without hope of coming together again.

Example: When Martin dated Steve's girlfriend behind Steve's back, the two men's friendship was breached **irreparably**.

Synonym: irrevocably, hopelessly
Antonym: temporarily, momentarily

143.

Definition: Lamentably (*adv*): sadly; regrettably; sorrowfully.

Example: "**Lamentably**, because your paper was late, I am unable to give you a higher grade," the professor told the student.

Synonym: unfortunately
Antonym: fortunately

144.

Definition: Laudably (*adv*): praiseworthily; admirably.

Example: The bystanders behaved **laudably**; they jumped right in to help the victim.

Synonym: commendably
Antonym: dishonorably

145. *Word Knowledge*

Officiously

146. *Word Knowledge*

Perpetually

147. *Word Knowledge*

Potently

145.

Definition: Officiously (*adv*): behaving obtrusively; behaving with interference and intervention when they are not called for.

Example: Seeing the well-dressed waiter in the fancy restaurant trying to direct what his daughter ordered, the father spoke up and said, "You are behaving **officiously**; my daughter will eat what she likes."

Synonym: intrusively
Antonym: tactfully

146.

Definition: Perpetually (*adv*): going on forever; never-ending; doing the same thing again and again.

Example: "He is **perpetually** complaining about everything," said the boss, "and I cannot promote someone with that kind of an attitude."

Synonym: perennially, constantly
Antonym: inconstantly, seldom

147.

Definition: Potently (*adv*): with power; with strength behind it; forcefully.

Example: The two medicines she was prescribed mixed **potently** to make her feel better within hours.

Synonym: powerfully, effectively
Antonym: impotently, ineffectively

148. *Word Knowledge*

Pugnaciously

149. *Word Knowledge*

Relentlessly

150. *Word Knowledge*

Ruefully

148. *Word Knowledge*

Definition: Pugnaciously (*adv*): willing to fight; with a chip on one's shoulder; wanting to spark conflict.

Example: Their friend Jim was acting so **pugnaciously** after a couple of drinks, the group tried to take him home before he could pick a fight with someone.

Synonym: belligerently, argumentatively
Antonym: pacifically, calmly

---

149. *Word Knowledge*

Definition: Relentlessly (*adv*): without ceasing or respite; without stopping or softening.

Example: They way he **relentlessly** studied, he could not fail but to get top grades.

Synonym: unremittingly, incessantly
Antonym: intermittently, occasionally

---

150. *Word Knowledge*

Definition: Ruefully (*adv*): regretfully; wishing one hadn't.

Example: "I didn't apologize," Joy said **ruefully**, "and now it is too late."

Synonym: penitently
Antonym: proudly

151. *Word Knowledge*

Sedulously

152. *Word Knowledge*

Tersely

153. *Word Knowledge*

Ultimately

151.

Definition: Sedulously (*adv*): done with hard work; done with concentration.

Example: I had **sedulously** prepared for my speech and it helped me feel confident as I approached the podium.

Synonym: assiduously
Antonym: lazily, carelessly

152.

Definition: Tersely (*adv*): shortly; with as few words as possible; in a condensed manner.

Example: Some men tend to speak **tersely**, which makes for frustration among expressive women.

Synonym: succinctly
Antonym: eloquently

153.

Definition: Ultimately (*adv*): finally; in the last analysis; at the end; at the finish.

Example: Ultimately, Gina hopes to be a published writer, so she is majoring in literature now.

Synonym: lastly
Antonym: firstly, incipiently

154. *Word Knowledge*

Unscrupulously

155. *Word Knowledge*

Voraciously

154.   *Word Knowledge*

Definition: Unscrupulously (*adv*): without scruple; without principles; immorally.

Example: The seller **unscrupulously** kept certain facts from the buyer—like the fact that the basement of the house leaked rivers every time it rained.

Synonym: dishonestly
Antonym: honestly

155.   *Word Knowledge*

Definition: Voraciously (*adv*): with great appetite; devouring with great eagerness.

Example: Because he used to go to the library and read **voraciously**, it is no wonder he won so much money on *Jeopardy*.

Synonym: ravenously
Antonym: disinterestedly

156. General Dan Sickles was a "political general" during the Civil War, receiving his command through influence rather than military training. At the Battle of Gettysburg, Sickles moved his troops forward, leaving the left flank of the Union army exposed. Most historians agree that this nearly cost the Union the battle. After the war Sickles used his political influence to preserve the battlefield as a historical landmark. As a result, Sickles is sometimes known as the general who nearly lost the battle but saved the battlefield.

Why is the fact that Dan Sickles was a "political general" important in this paragraph?

A. His political skills worked both for and against him regarding Gettysburg
B. Political generals think strategically
C. Sickles made his move in a bid for fame, glory, and to be elected president
D. The political atmosphere of the time required generals to take bold initiatives

---

157. Many people have blamed the White Star Line for the loss of life suffered on the *RMS Titanic*. Even though the *Titanic* carried more lifeboats than was legally required, the owners did not provide enough lifeboats for every person on board. Lifeboats were to be used again and again to ferry passengers from the sinking ship to a rescue ship. Unfortunately, the nearest ship to answer *Titanic's* distress signals was too far away to prevent the loss of over a thousand lives.

What is the perspective of the author of this paragraph?

A. The White Star Line only carried enough lifeboats to rescue first class passengers.
B. The White Star Line kept third class passengers behind gates and prevented their evacuation of the ship.
C. The White Star Line did not deliberately act irresponsibly on the matter of lifeboats.
D. Lifeboats were kept to a minimum to clear up deck space for the rich to promenade.

---

158. Marie and Pierre Curie devoted their lives to the discovery of elements, including polonium and radium. United by love of science and one another, they spent romantic evenings gazing at the glow of the radium in the beakers in their laboratory. Unfortunately, they knew little of the power of radiation, and handling it affected their health. Scientists still cannot open the notebooks of this dedicated couple because they are covered with radiation.

What is the topic sentence of this paragraph?

A. Scientists still cannot open the notebooks of this dedicated couple because they are covered with radiation.
B. Marie and Pierre Curie devoted their lives to the discovery of elements, including polonium and radium.
C. Unfortunately, they knew little of the power of radiation, and handling it affected their health.
D. United by love of science and one another, they spent romantic evenings gazing at the glow of the radium in the beakers in their laboratory.

156.

Answer: A. His political skills worked both for and against him regarding Gettysburg

A is the correct answer because it correctly states the main point of the paragraph: that his political skills worked both for and against him. His political influence helped him secure a prestigious commission as general and after the war it helped him in the fight to preserve the battlefield, but he gained a position through political influence that he wasn't qualified to hold, and this inexperience nearly cost the Union the battle.

157.

Answer: C. The White Star Line did not deliberately act irresponsibly on the matter of lifeboats.

C is the correct answer because it summarizes the point of the paragraph without bringing in information not provided within the paragraph itself. The author makes a point to note that the owners followed the legal requirements and that the *Titanic* was too far from help to save everyone on board. This indicates that the author does not hold the owners of the *Titanic* responsible.

158.

Answer: B. Marie and Pierre Curie devoted their lives to the discovery of elements, including polonium and radium.

B is the correct answer because it states the subject of the paragraph. A sentence that does this is called the topic sentence. A topic sentence usually appears at the beginning of a paragraph, but it can also be the last sentence. No matter where a topic sentence appears, it states the general topic of the paragraph and all other sentences relate to, expand on, and/or support it.

159. Some critics question whether reality TV is good for society. They point out that reality TV contestants audition for their roles and are always aware that the camera is on them. Are their actions and responses real or acted? Fans may love and vote for a contestant, thinking they know and care about that person, not realizing that it is all a carefully scripted front. Critics wonder if reality TV is not a substitute for genuine compassion for other people.

Which of the following sentences best summarizes the paragraph?

A. Reality TV should be banned from television.
B. People who watch reality TV are uncaring people.
C. Reality TV is such that viewers who think they truly care about the contestants may not really know the contestants at all.
D. Contestants on reality TV shows are paid actors and their stories are fraudulent.

---

160. During the Salem Witch Trials of 1692, nineteen adults were executed for allegedly practicing witchcraft. During these trials, spectral evidence was allowed into court testimony as if it were fact. Spectral evidence meant dreams, visions, suspicions, and feelings. Fortunately, officials realized that spectral evidence was not proof, and when it was finally barred from the courtroom, the executions ceased.

From the context of this paragraph, the word "allegedly" may be understood to mean what?

A. It means practicing activities that are "on the edge".
B. It means doing something mentally unbalanced; it has the same Latin root as the word ledger.
C. It means "supposedly" or what people said they did; it describes unproven assertions.
D. It is a synonym for "allowing". The accused tolerated the practice of witchcraft in their homes and on their farms.

---

161. To accomplish something exceptional requires numerous virtues of character: will power, determination, perseverance, and courage, among others. Edmund Hillary of New Zealand (1919-2008) was the first human being to reach the top of Mount Everest, an elevation of 30,000 feet. He was very proud, but when he heard that some modern climbers did not stop their ascent of Everest to help a dying man, he was angry that people valued their own achievements over helping a fellow human being.

What can be inferred from the above paragraph?

A. Climbing Mount Everest is not a worthy endeavor.
B. Unbridled ambition characterizes the modern age.
C. Edmund Hillary wanted his achievement to stand alone against all challengers.
D. Edmund Hillary was a man of will power, determination, perseverance, courage, and compassion.

159. *Paragraph Comprehension*

Answer: C. Reality TV is such that viewers who think they truly care about the contestants may not really know the contestants at all.

C is the correct answer because it states in shortened form (i.e., summarizes) the main point of the paragraph. The paragraph itself does not draw conclusions about reality TV, it merely raises questions, using such phrases as "critics question" or "critics wonder". C is the most accurate summary of the paragraph and, like the paragraph, it does not draw conclusions.

160. *Paragraph Comprehension*

Answer: C. It means "supposedly" or what people said they did; it describes unproven assertions.

C is the correct answer and is clearly supported by the context of the paragraph. The paragraph clearly implies that the evidence brought against those who were executed was so questionable, it was eventually not admitted in court. Therefore, the accusations of practicing witchcraft were simply what people thought or said about the executed—what they supposedly did, or what others asserted they did without any kind of real proof.

161. *Paragraph Comprehension*

Answer: D. Edmund Hillary was a man of will power, determination, perseverance, courage, and compassion.

D is the correct answer because in being the first person to scale Mount Everest, Edmund Hillary clearly possessed the virtues listed at the beginning of the paragraph. While other climbers also have these virtues, some of them were lacking in compassion because they bypassed a dying man in order to get to the top. From his anger about this, it can be inferred that Hillary also possessed the virtue of compassion. There is no evidence or implication in the paragraph that the other answers are true. The other answers draw conclusions and make judgments that are not implied in the paragraph.

162. Historically, the medical community has been slow to welcome change. Bleeding—the medieval method of removing disease by letting out large quantities of blood—was still being practiced in nineteenth century America. When Dr. Semmelweis of Hungary reduced hospital deaths by nearly ten percent in the 1840s by asking hospital personnel to sanitize their hands, he was hounded out of his practice and his sanity by the medical community of his time.

What is the main theme of the paragraph?

A. Dr. Semmelweis was an unsung hero.
B. The medical community in the past was highly resistant to change.
C. Washing one's hands should be basic medical procedure.
D. Bleeding had its good points and bad points.

163. People who live to be 100 years or older are called centenarians. Worldwide, more and more people are reaching this landmark age. The average life span is increasing because of improved nutrition, medicine, and basic health practices; however, most centenarians share two important characteristics with one another: 1) they eat healthy diets and 2) they manage stress well.

What point can be inferred from the paragraph above?

A. Life style factors are strong predictors of longevity.
B. Living longer is genetically determined.
C. Centenarians are so diverse that their longevity seems to be a matter of luck.
D. Few people reach the age of 100 and fewer still will reach it in the future.

164. Ernest Shackleton was a twentieth century British arctic explorer. On one trip to Antarctica, Shackleton's ship broke into splinters while trapped in packed ocean ice. Shackleton and his crew camped for almost two years on the ice, eating penguins. Shackleton then took a small boat over 800 miles of ocean and crossed snow-covered mountain peaks on foot to find rescue. He saved all twenty-eight of his crew members. His name is synonymous with the name of his ship: *Endurance*.

What is the main topic of this paragraph?

A. Ernest Shackleton
B. Antarctic exploration
C. Arctic survival and endurance
D. The dangers of ocean travel in arctic seas

162. *Paragraph Comprehension*

Answer: B. The medical community in the past was highly resistant to change.

B is the correct answer because it accurately restates the topic sentence of the paragraph (the first sentence), which lays out the main theme. All of the supporting sentences back up that main theme by providing supporting details. If the medical community of the time had not been resistant to change, then they would have welcomed Dr. Semmelweis' ideas instead of driving him out of the practice of medicine.

163. *Paragraph Comprehension*

Answer: A. Life style factors are strong predictors of longevity.

A is the correct answer because it correctly infers from the information in the paragraph that longevity is related to lifestyle. Answers B, C, and D are not supported by the information in the paragraph, therefore the inferences they make are not accurate, at least as far as the information presented in this paragraph goes. Answer A is also the only answer that does not bring in extraneous information that is not in the paragraph.

164. *Paragraph Comprehension*

Answer: A. Ernest Shackleton

A is the correct answer because the paragraph focuses on the deeds and character of Ernest Shackleton. The first sentence is about Ernest Shackleton, indicating that the paragraph is about him. Other information and background in the paragraph all serve to support the paragraph's message of Shackleton's leadership and character in a survival situation. Antarctica and arctic conditions and dangers set the scene and are the background for Shackleton's heroism; they are secondary topics rather than the main topic.

165. The development of culture has often ridden on the back of trade. In ancient times a series of trade routes called The Silk Road went from China to what is now Europe, traversing five thousand miles. Silk, gold and other precious metals, ivory, glass, fur, jade, bronze and iron were exchanged. In addition, ideas, philosophies, customs, technological innovations, and even religions traveled along the Silk Road and helped to develop civilization.

What is the topic sentence in this paragraph?

A. In ancient times a series of trade routes called "The Silk Road" went from China to what is now Europe, traversing five thousand miles.
B. The development of culture has often ridden on the back of trade.
C. Silk, gold and other precious metals, ivory, glass, fur, jade, bronze and iron were exchanged.
D. In addition, ideas, philosophies, customs, technological innovations and even religions traveled along the Silk Road and helped to develop civilization.

166. According to the Centers for Disease Control (CDC) and the National Institutes of Health (NIH), half the adult population of the United States is obese. Obese people are at increased risk for coronary heart disease, diabetes, cancer, liver and gallbladder diseases, and other health problems. These sources further state that about 10% of total U.S. health expenditures go to obesity-related issues.

Why is this paragraph different from an editorial or opinion piece?

A. The paragraph takes the point of view that obesity is unhealthy.
B. The paragraph was probably written by a non-obese person.
C. The paragraph only cites facts from well-known and reliable sources.
D. The paragraph shows strong bias against obese people.

167. *American Idol* has been one of the greatest ratings giants in the history of American television. Some predicted that when the original trio of judges—Randy Jackson, Simon Cowell, and Paula Abdul—broke up, the show would lose its ratings. During a transitional season, ratings did fall, but with three solid judges in place—Jennifer Lopez, Randy Jackson, and Steven Tyler—the televised singing contest is once again on the top of the heap.

What quality does the paragraph imply about the show *American Idol*?

A. It is reminiscent.
B. It is resilient.
C. It has forbearance.
D. It is raucous.

165.

Answer: B. The development of culture has often ridden on the back of trade.

B is the correct answer because it is the first sentence of the paragraph (the usual place for a topic sentence) and it states the main idea of the paragraph. The paragraph is not only about the Silk Road and what traveled along it. The paragraph is about how the trade route led to cultural exchange and therefore development.

166.

Answer: C. The paragraph only cites facts from well-known and reliable sources.

C is the correct answer because the paragraph is based entirely upon facts from the CDC and NIH. An opinion piece may also use facts to support its arguments, but an opinion piece or editorial will also state a position based upon selected facts. This paragraph states no position. Each sentence simply contains information, without additional comment, taken from the CDC and NIH.

167.

Answer: B. It is resilient.

B is the correct answer because the paragraph's description of *American Idol's* ability to bounce back from setback fits the definition of the word resilient. According to the paragraph, the show has experienced its ups and downs, including major changes in the judging line-up, but in the long run the show has made up for its losses due to such changes and regained its high ratings.

168. Since DNA testing became accepted in the 1980s as conclusive evidence, groups like Project Innocence have sprung up. These groups aim to prove that some people who have been incarcerated for years are innocent of the crimes they were convicted of. Project Innocence maintains that people are often convicted on the basis of eyewitness testimony, and that 75% of the convictions that are overturned through DNA testing were based on eyewitness misidentification.

Based on the paragraph, what does the phrase "conclusive evidence" in the first sentence mean?

A. Evidence that comes in at the end of a trial by jury
B. Evidence that is most likely accurate
C. Evidence that is given during the prosecuting attorney's closing
D. Evidence that cannot be argued with

169. The royal Romanov family of Russia was executed when the Red Army took over the country in 1918. For decades, impostors appeared, claiming to be the youngest princess, Anastasia. Anastasia was only seventeen at the time of the killings and supposedly escaped. The mystery deepened when the royal family's bones were exhumed and one princess's skeleton was missing. By 2008, however, Anastasia's bones were located, and at last the fate of all the members of the royal family was known.

Using the entire context of the paragraph, what does the word "impostor" mean?

A. Someone falsely claiming the identity of another person.
B. Someone who imitates other people to make a living as a comic.
C. Someone who is impossible to deal with because of lack of truthfulness.
D. Someone who really is a famous person but no one realizes it.

170. The Internet has revolutionized many industries in the world, shrinking the world into the so-called global village. Business may now operate virtually with teams of people working together while on opposite sides of the globe. The Internet has also made the world more transparent as people post information about products, services, and the corporations that provide them. The Internet promotes democracy as people express themselves openly and exercise the power of public opinion.

What words best describe the author's attitude toward the Internet?

A. Neutral
B. Positive
C. Negative
D. Cautious

168. *Paragraph Comprehension*

Answer: D. Evidence that cannot be argued with

D is the correct answer because something that is conclusive means that there are no more believable arguments against it. When something comes to its conclusion that means that there is no more to be said. DNA testing is considered so accurate, it may be considered unarguable proof; therefore, it is conclusive evidence.

169. *Paragraph Comprehension*

Answer: A. Someone falsely claiming the identity of another person.

A is the correct answer because the context of the paragraph shows that Anastasia died with her family in 1918. In spite of rumors that she escaped and a missing skeleton when the bodies were exhumed, conclusive evidence in 2008 showed that Anastasia was indeed among the executed royal family members. Therefore, any claims otherwise had to be false. Any person claiming to be Anastasia could not possibly be so, and so had to be making a false claim on Anastasia's identity.

170. *Paragraph Comprehension*

Answer: B. Positive

B is the correct answer because the paragraph has a tone of excitement about the potential of this technology. "Revolutionizing" industries, "shrinking" the world into a village, "exercising" the power of public opinion are all active verbs that imply motion in a positive and exciting new direction.

171. Jane Austen's book *Sense and Sensibility* provides a contrast between two sisters' approaches to love. Elinor is self-controlled and masks her emotions, even when the man she loves appears to have betrayed her. She represents "sense." Her sister Marianne is ruled by "sensibility" or emotion. Marianne carries on shamelessly about an unworthy man. Everyone in London and the countryside knows exactly how Marianne feels. The book turns out happily for both sisters once they learn to balance reason and emotion.

According to the paragraph, what does Jane Austen's *Sense and Sensibility* contrast?

A. Love versus infatuation
B. Steadfastness versus timelessness
C. Head versus heart
D. Sensibility versus sensitivity

---

172. Two famous wilderness stories teach how important it is to have a partner. Jack London's *To Build a Fire* tells of a man hiking in the Klondike who proudly thinks he can make it alone. The more recent movie *127 Hours* tells of how mountain climber Aron Ralston got his arm hopelessly trapped under a boulder and how his lone wolf tendencies brought him to this pass. Both men suffer tragedy due to their solitary ways.

Which answer best describes the author's point of view in this paragraph?

A. Rugged individualism is a desirable trait.
B. People need one another to survive and thrive.
C. In the wilderness, partnership is important but not in other walks of life.
D. In survival situations, the only person to be relied upon is one's self.

---

173. Humans can train wild animals to an extraordinary degree. Anyone who has ever enjoyed the Orca (killer whale) show at Sea World must marvel at the beautiful rapport between the 12,000 pound whales and their trainers. Likewise, Siegfried and Roy's white tiger shows in Las Vegas were megahits with audiences. However, the drowning of killer whale trainer Dawn Brancheau and the mauling of Roy by a 600 pound tiger show that these fascinating animals remain dangerous even to expert trainers.

From the context of the paragraph, what does the word "rapport" in the second sentence mean?

A. Communication, synchrony, and understanding
B. Dominance-submission dynamic
C. Discipline by rapping with a rod
D. Wrapping the animal's nose in a special cord that vibrates electronic commands that the animal understands

171.   *Paragraph Comprehension*

Answer: C. Head versus heart

C is the correct answer because it parallels the contrasts spelled out in the paragraph. This contrast is stated directly in the last sentence as reason versus emotion and in the body of the paragraph with contrasting examples of the sister's behavior. The paragraph speaks of Elinor's self-control and ability to conceal her emotions as opposed to Marianne's emotionalism and public displays, describing a contrast between being ruled by the head versus the heart.

172.   *Paragraph Comprehension*

Answer: B. People need one another to survive and thrive.

B is the correct answer because the author continually emphasizes how not relying on other people leads to tragic consequences. The author explains how difficult it is to "make it alone" or "go it alone" or be a "lone wolf" with "solitary ways" when it comes to avoiding severe difficulty, thus strongly implying the need for partnership in survival situations and beyond.

173.   *Paragraph Comprehension*

Answer: A. Communication, synchrony, and understanding

A is the correct answer because the context of the paragraph makes it clear that the rapport between the trainers and animals is beautiful and that audiences marvel at it. It would not be a marvel if trainers simply dominated the animals through force or instruments. A good relationship is characterized by communication, synchrony, and understanding. As the last sentence implies, if a wild animal does not want to obey its trainer, no amount of force or device available to a trainer can avoid tragedy.

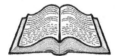

174. Angelina Jolie is one of the most admired women in the world, yet she has confided that she suffered from low self-esteem and isolation as a teenager. Growing up with a single mother, she lacked funds to dress fashionably, and she was derided by classmates because of her unusual facial features and nonconformity. If even great movie stars suffer anomie, it is natural that average teenagers sometimes feel that way too.

From the context of the paragraph, what does the word "anomie" in the last sentence mean?

A. Anonymity, anomalies, relativity
B. Adolescent angst, acne, attitude
C. Anger at being bullied
D. Uncertainty, unresolved identity issues, alienation

175. Ice Hotel in Sweden is close to the Arctic Circle. Chandeliers, beds, decorative sculptures and chambers are all made of ice—even the drinking glasses are made of ice. However, hotel guests are given plenty of warm liquids, furs, and insulation to keep them warm as they sleep in the subzero temperatures. The scintillating beauty of fire and candle among the ice structures makes for a reflective experience in the silence of the arctic night.

From the context of the last sentence of the paragraph, does the phrase "reflective experience" refer to the literal reflection of fire and ice?

A. Yes, it refers to the literal reflection of fire, flame, and ice.
B. No, it refers to contemplation inspired by beauty, contrast, and silence.
C. No, it refers to how the firelight and flame reflect on the features of others in cozy chats around the fireside.
D. Yes, because the ice would slowly melt in such a setting and create reflecting pools of light.

174. *Paragraph Comprehension*

Answer: D. Uncertainty, unresolved identity issues, alienation

D is the most complete and accurate answer. The paragraph says that Jolie suffered from low self-esteem, isolation, being made fun of, and feeling different from others. Her low self-esteem implies uncertainty about herself, which would mean unresolved identity issues. Being derided, as the paragraph says she was, because of being different would result in a sense of isolation and of being a stranger. These are feelings of alienation.

175. *Paragraph Comprehension*

Answer: B. No, it refers to contemplation inspired by beauty, contrast, and silence.

B is the correct answer because the use of words like "beauty" and "silence of the arctic night," as well as the tone of the sentence, implies a contemplative (reflective) state inspired, in part, by the contrast of fire, light and ice in the unusual setting. A literal experience of seeing the reflection of light and ice would not involve such poetic and dramatic language.

176.

Adding and Subtracting Fractions

177.

Common Denominators

178.

Multiplying and Dividing Fractions

176.

For addition or subtraction of rational fractions, the numerators can be added or subtracted **only** when the denominators are equal.

$$\frac{1}{5} + \frac{2}{5} = \frac{1+2}{5} = \frac{3}{5}$$

If the denominators are different, find the least common denominator and convert the fractions appropriately. See Common Denominators flashcard.

$$\frac{2}{3} - \frac{1}{9} = \left(\frac{2}{3} \times \frac{3}{3}\right) - \frac{1}{9} = \frac{6}{9} - \frac{1}{9} = \frac{6-1}{9} = \frac{5}{9}$$

177.

The least common denominator (LCD) is the smallest number into which each denominator will divide evenly.

Example: 2/3 – 1/2 (the least common denominator is 6)

Once the LCD is determined, express each fraction in terms of the LCD. This is done by multiplying both the numerator and denominator of each fraction by whatever number is required to make its denominator the same value as the LCD.

Example: (2/2)(2/3) – (1/2)(3/3) = 4/6 – 3/6 = 1/6

178.

For multiplication of two fractions, the result is simply the product of the numerators over the product of the denominators.

$$\frac{3}{4} \times \frac{1}{7} = \frac{3 \times 1}{4 \times 7} = \frac{3}{28}$$

Division involves multiplication by the reciprocal of the divisor.

$$\frac{4}{5} \div \frac{7}{2} = \frac{4}{5} \times \frac{2}{7} = \frac{8}{35}$$

179. *Mathematics Knowledge*

Simplify: $\dfrac{1}{6} + \dfrac{4}{5} - \dfrac{3}{4}$

A. 13/60
B. 2/7
C. 7/30
D. 2/15

180. *Mathematics Knowledge*

After a party, there was $\dfrac{1}{5}$ of one pizza and $\dfrac{2}{3}$ of another pizza of the same size left over. What fraction of a whole pizza was left over altogether?

A. 3/8
B. 13/15
C. 3/15
D. 3/5

181. *Mathematics Knowledge*

If 5 people share $\dfrac{3}{4}$ of a pizza, what fraction of a whole pizza will each person get?

A. 3/5
B. 1/15
C. 3/20
D. 3/15

179.

Answer: A. 13/60

Before adding or subtracting the numerators, a common denominator must be found. The least common denominator for 4, 5, and 6 is 60. Expressing each term as a fraction of 60 gives:

$$\frac{1}{6}+\frac{4}{5}-\frac{3}{4}=\frac{10}{60}+\frac{48}{60}-\frac{45}{60}=\frac{13}{60}$$

180.

Answer: B. 13/15

Before adding 1/5 and 2/3, a common denominator must be found. The least common denominator for 5 and 3 is 15. Expressing each term as a fraction of 15 gives:

$$\frac{1}{5}+\frac{2}{3}=\frac{3}{15}+\frac{10}{15}=\frac{13}{15}$$

181.

Answer: C. 3/20

Dividing a fraction by a number (in this case, the number 5) can be done by multiplying the fraction by the reciprocal of that number (the reciprocal of 5 is 1/5).

$$\frac{3}{4}\div5=\frac{3}{4}\times\frac{1}{5}=\frac{3}{20}$$

182. *Mathematics Knowledge*

Simplify: $\left(\dfrac{1}{3}\times\dfrac{2}{5}\right)+\left(\dfrac{4}{5}\times\dfrac{4}{9}\right)$

A. 22/45
B. 10/45
C. 10/15
D. 14/15

---

183. *Mathematics Knowledge*

Simplify: $\left(\dfrac{1}{2}+\dfrac{2}{5}\right)\div\left(\dfrac{1}{4}+\dfrac{3}{5}\right)$

A. 18/17
B. 153/200
C. 17/18
D. 1/5

---

184. *Mathematics Knowledge*

Emily spent $\dfrac{3}{4}$ hour doing her English homework, $\dfrac{2}{3}$ hour on math and $\dfrac{1}{6}$ hour on civics. How much time did she spend in all doing her homework?

A. 1 hour 7 minutes
B. 1 hour 35 minutes
C. 1 hour 19 minutes
D. 1 hour 17 minutes

182.

Answer: A. 22/45

First perform the calculations inside of the parentheses. Then express each fraction in terms of a common denominator before adding them.

$$\left(\frac{1}{3}\times\frac{2}{5}\right)+\left(\frac{4}{5}\times\frac{4}{9}\right)=\frac{2}{15}+\frac{16}{45}=\frac{6}{45}+\frac{16}{45}=\frac{22}{45}$$

183.

Answer: A. 18/17

First perform the calculations inside of the parentheses. Each set of fractions will need to be expressed in terms of a common denominator before performing the addition. Then perform the division by multiplying by the reciprocal.

$$\left(\frac{1}{2}+\frac{2}{5}\right)\div\left(\frac{1}{4}+\frac{3}{5}\right)=\left(\frac{5}{10}+\frac{4}{10}\right)\div\left(\frac{5}{20}+\frac{12}{20}\right)=$$

$$\frac{9}{10}\div\frac{17}{20}=\frac{9}{10}\times\frac{20}{17}=\frac{18}{17}$$

184.

Answer: B. 1 hour 35 minutes

Before adding 3/4, 2/3, and 1/6, a common denominator must be found. The least common denominator for 4, 3, and 6 is 12. Expressing each term as a fraction of 12 gives:

$$\frac{3}{4}+\frac{2}{3}+\frac{1}{6}=\frac{9}{12}+\frac{8}{12}+\frac{2}{12}=\frac{19}{12}=1\frac{7}{12}$$

$$\frac{7}{12}\text{ of an hour = }\frac{7}{12}\times 60=35\text{ minutes.}$$

So the total time Emily spent on homework is 1 hour 35 minutes.

185.

0.625 is equivalent to:

A. 7/9
B. 3/8
C. 5/8
D. 6/9

186.

Adding and Subtracting Negative Numbers

187.

Multiplying and Dividing Negative Numbers

185.

Mathematics Knowledge

Answer: C. 5/8

To change a decimal into a fraction, write the decimal part of the number as the fraction's numerator. For the fraction's denominator, use the place value represented by the last number in the decimal. Reduce the resulting fraction as far as possible.

Place value: 0.625 (6 represents the tenths place value, 2 represents the hundredths place value, 5 represents the thousandths place value, etc.)

$$0.625 = \frac{625}{1000} = \frac{25}{40} = \frac{5}{8}$$

186.

Mathematics Knowledge

<u>Adding two negative numbers</u>: This is the same as adding positive numbers except the result is negative: (-4) + (-6) = -10
<u>Adding positive and negative numbers</u>: Think of the negative number as a positive number being subtracted: (-3 + 11) = (11 − 3) = 8 If the negative number is larger, the result will be negative: 5 + (-19) = (5 − 19) = -14

<u>Subtracting a positive number</u>: Think of it as adding a negative number: (-5 − 1) = (-5) + (-1) = -6 Another example: (-2 − 6) = (-2) + (-6) = -8
<u>Subtracting a negative number</u>: Think of it as adding a positive number: 7 − (-3) = 7 + 3 = 10 Another example: -5 − (-12) = -5 + 12 = 7

187.

Mathematics Knowledge

The same rules apply for both multiplying and dividing negative numbers:

One positive number and one negative number will give a negative result.
5 x (-5) = -25
10 ÷ (-2) = -5

Two negative numbers will give a positive result.
-2 x (-2) = 4
-15 ÷ (-3) = 5

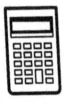

188. *Mathematics Knowledge*

Simplify: $(-5+11) \div (-2-1)$

A. -2
B. 2
C. 6
D. -6

---

189. *Mathematics Knowledge*

Mike's dad is 40 years old. Mike tells a friend that his sister's age is 6 years less than one-eighth his dad's age. Can he be right? Why or why not?

A. Yes, since Mike claims his sister is 1 year old
B. Yes, since Mike claims his sister is 5 years old
C. No, since Mike claims his sister is -1 year old
D. No, since Mike claims his sister is -5 year old

---

190. *Mathematics Knowledge*

Simplify: $\dfrac{(0.65-2.15) \times (5.5-6.25)}{(4.5-3.0)}$

A. 1.4
B. -1.5
C. -0.75
D. 0.75

188. *Mathematics Knowledge*

Answer: A. -2

$$(-5+11) \div (-2-1) = 6 \div (-3) = -2$$

189. *Mathematics Knowledge*

Answer: C. No, since Mike claims his sister is -1 year old

Six years less than 1/8 Mike's dad's age = (40/8) − 6 = 5 − 6 = -1

190. *Mathematics Knowledge*

Answer: D. 0.75

$$\frac{(0.65-2.15) \times (5.5-6.25)}{(4.5-3.0)} = \frac{(-1.5) \times (-0.75)}{1.5} = 0.75$$

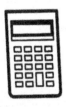

191.

Evaluate $4 \div 2 \times (7 - 3) \times 6 - (8 - 5)$

A. -10
B. 45
C. 0
D. 15

192.

Evaluate $2^3 \div 4 \times (7 + 3)^2 \times 6$

A. 1200
B. 3/25
C. 192
D. 1500

193.

13^0 is equal to:

A. 13
B. 1
C. 0
D. 130

191.

Answer: B. 45

Follow the PEMDAS rule: **P**arenthesis, **E**xponent, **M**ultiplication and **D**ivision from left to right, followed by **A**ddition and **S**ubtraction from left to right.

For this problem, do the operations in parentheses first, then division and multiplication from left to right followed by subtraction.

$4 \div 2 \times (7 - 3) \times 6 - (8 - 5) = 4 \div 2 \times 4 \times 6 - 3 =$
$2 \times 4 \times 6 - 3 = 48 - 3 = 45$

192.

Answer: A. 1200

Follow the PEMDAS rule: **P**arenthesis, **E**xponent, **M**ultiplication and **D**ivision from left to right, followed by **A**ddition and **S**ubtraction from left to right.

For this problem, do the operation in the parenthesis first then evaluate exponents, followed by division and multiplication from left to right.

$2^3 \div 4 \times (7 + 3)^2 \times 6 = 2^3 \div 4 \times 10^2 \times 6 = 8 \div 4 \times 100 \times 6 =$
$2 \times 100 \times 6 = 1200$

193.

Answer: B. 1

Any number raised to the power zero is equal to one. This is easy to understand if one thinks of a number raised to any power divided by itself:

$$\frac{13^5}{13^5} = 13^{5-5} = 13^0 = 1$$

194.

Solve for x:
52 - 3x = 4

A. 16
B. 48
C. -16
D. 56/3

195.

Solve for x:
7x +5 − 2x = 15

A. 10/9
B. 4
C. 2
D. 20/9

196.

Solve for x:
3x + 7 = 22 − 2x

A. 15
B. 3
C. 29
D. 29/5

194.

Answer: A. 16

To solve the equation 52 - 3x = 4, first subtract 52 from both sides:
-3x = -48

Then divide both sides by -3:
x = 16

195.

Answer: C. 2

To solve the equation 7x +5 – 2x = 15, first combine the two x terms on the left hand side of the equation:
5x + 5 = 15

Then subtract 5 from both sides to get:
5x = 10

Divide both sides by 5:
x = 2

196.

Answer: B. 3

To solve the equation 3x + 7 = 22 – 2x, first add 2x to both sides in order to have x on just one side of the equation:
5x + 7 = 22

Subtract 7 from both sides:
5x = 15

Divide both sides by 5:
x = 3

197.

Evaluate $2x^2 - 3x + xy - y^2$ when x = -1 and y = 2

A. -7
B. -1
C. -3
D. 3

198.

Solve for y:
3y + 2x = y + 3

A. (2x − 3)/3
B. 3 − 2x
C. 3 − x
D. (3 − 2x)/2

199.

Solve for y:
2ax + 3by = c

A. (c − 2ax)/3b
B. (c − 3b)/2ax
C. (2ax − c)/3b
D. (2ax + c)/3b

197.

Answer: B. -1

Substituting the values x = -1 and y = 2 in the expression we get:

$2x^2 - 3x + xy - y^2 = 2(-1)^2 - 3(-1) + (-1)(2) - (2)^2 = 2 + 3 - 2 - 4 = -1$

198.

Answer: D. (3 – 2x)/2

To solve 3y + 2x = y + 3 for y, first combine both y terms by subtracting y from both sides:
2y + 2x = 3

Subtract 2x from both sides to isolate the y term:
2y = 3 – 2x

Divide both sides by 2:
y = (3 – 2x)/2

199.

Answer: A. (c – 2ax)/3b

To solve 2ax + 3by = c for y, first isolate the y term by subtracting 2ax from both   sides:
3by = c – 2ax

Divide both sides by 3b to get:
y = (c – 2ax)/3b

200. *Mathematics Knowledge*

Factor: $9x^2 - 16y^2$

A. $144(x - y)(x + y)$
B. $(3x - 4y)(3x + 4y)$
C. $(9x - 16y)(9x + 16y)$
D. Cannot be factored

201. *Mathematics Knowledge*

Solve for x by factoring:
$x^2 - 2x - 3 = 0$

A. $(1, -3)$
B. $(1, 3)$
C. $(-1, -3)$
D. $(-1, 3)$

202. *Mathematics Knowledge*

Solve for x and y by substitution:
$3x - y = 5$
$2x + 2y = 6$

A. $(1, 2)$
B. $(1, 3)$
C. $(2, 1)$
D. $(-1, 3)$

200.   *Mathematics Knowledge*

Answer: B. (3x – 4y)(3x + 4y)

$9x^2 - 16y^2 = (3x)^2 - (4y)^2 = (3x - 4y)(3x + 4y)$ using the formula $a^2 - b^2 = (a - b)(a + b)$

---

201.   *Mathematics Knowledge*

Answer: D. (-1, 3)

To solve $x^2 - 2x - 3 = 0$, first factor the expression on the left. Express the middle term 2x as 3x – x:
$x^2 - 3x + x - 3 = 0$

Factor by grouping:
$x^2 - 3x + x - 3 = x(x - 3) + 1(x - 3) = (x + 1)(x - 3) = 0$

Hence x + 1=0 or x – 3 = 0 and the two possible values of x = -1 and 3.

---

202.   *Mathematics Knowledge*

Answer: C. (2, 1)

Find y in terms of x from the first equation by subtracting 3x from both sides:
-y = 5 – 3x; y = 3x – 5

Substitute this expression for y in the second equation:
2x +2(3x – 5) = 6

Simplifying: 2x + 6x – 10 = 6; 8x –10 = 6

Adding 10 to both sides and then dividing both sides by 2:
8x = 16;   x = 2

Substituting this value of x in the first equation:
3(2) – y = 5;   6 – y = 5;   -y = -1; y = 1

203.   *Mathematics Knowledge*

Simplify: $(4xy^2z)(6x^3yz^4)$

A. $10x^2y^2z^2$

B. $24x^4y^3z^5$

C. $24x^3y^2z^4$

D. $4x^4y^3z^5$

---

204.   *Mathematics Knowledge*

Evaluate: (-6.35) x (-1.2)

A. -7.26

B. 762.0

C. 76.20

D. 7.620

---

205.   *Mathematics Knowledge*

Simplify: $a^2c\left(b^3c+ab\right)$

A. $a^2b^3c^2+a^3bc$

B. $a^5b^4c^3$

C. $a\,b^2c^2+a^2c$

D. $a^2b^3c^2$

203.   *Mathematics Knowledge*

Answer: B. $24x^4y^3z^5$

$$(4xy^2z)(6x^3yz^4) = (4 \times 6)(x \times x^3)(y^2 \times y)(z \times z^4) = 24x^4y^3z^5$$

---

204.   *Mathematics Knowledge*

Answer: D. 7.620

Since both numbers are negative, the answer will be positive.

First multiply 635 and 12: 635 x 12 = 7260.

Since there are 2 digits to the right of the decimal point in 6.35, and 1 digit to the right of the decimal point in 1.3, the answer should have 3 digits to the right of the decimal point.

Hence (-6.35) x (-1.2) = 7.260

---

205.   *Mathematics Knowledge*

Answer: A. $a^2b^3c^2 + a^3bc$

To evaluate $a^2c(b^3c + ab)$, first use the distributive law to simplify the expression:
$$a^2c(b^3c + ab) = (a^2c)(b^3c) + (a^2c)(ab)$$

For each term, combine like variables by adding exponents:
$$(a^2c)(b^3c) + (a^2c)(ab) = a^2b^3c^2 + a^3bc$$

206. *Mathematics Knowledge*

What is the next term in the series $\frac{7}{8}, 1\frac{1}{4}, 1\frac{5}{8}, 2, 2\frac{3}{8}, \ldots$?

A. $2\frac{3}{8}$

B. $2\frac{3}{4}$

C. $3\frac{1}{8}$

D. $3\frac{3}{4}$

---

207. *Mathematics Knowledge*

What is the square root of 144?

A. 12
B. 13
C. 9
D. 11

---

208. *Mathematics Knowledge*

Triangle ABC has sides that are 2cm, 5cm and 6cm long. Triangle DEF has sides that are 6cm, 15cm and 18cm long. The two triangles are:

A. Similar
B. Congruent
C. Similar and congruent
D. Neither similar nor congruent

206.   *Mathematics Knowledge*

Answer: B. $2\dfrac{3}{4}$

Express the series as terms with the common denominator 8:

$$\frac{7}{8}, \frac{10}{8}, \frac{13}{8}, \frac{16}{8}, \frac{19}{8}, \dots$$

It is clear that each term is $\dfrac{3}{8}$ more than the previous one.

Hence the next term in the series is $\dfrac{19}{8} + \dfrac{3}{8} = \dfrac{22}{8} = \dfrac{11}{4} = 2\dfrac{3}{4}$.

---

207.   *Mathematics Knowledge*

Answer: A. 12

Since 12 x 12 = 144, 12 is the square root of 144.

---

208.   *Mathematics Knowledge*

Answer: A. Similar

Two triangles are similar if they are the same in shape although they may be different in size. Mathematically, similarity of two triangles can be verified by showing that their corresponding sides are in proportion or that their corresponding angles are equal. In this case, $\dfrac{2}{6} = \dfrac{5}{15} = \dfrac{6}{18} = \dfrac{1}{3}$.

Since the sides of the two triangles are in the proportion 1:3, they are similar.

Since the lengths of their sides are not the same, they are not congruent.

209.   *Mathematics Knowledge*

Which of the following is not a parallelogram?

Square

Rectangle

Trapezoid

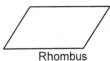
Rhombus

A. Square
B. Rectangle
C. Trapezoid
D. Rhombus

---

210.   *Mathematics Knowledge*

The difference between a rhombus and a square is that:

A. Only one of them has 4 equal sides
B. Only one of them has 2 sets of parallel sides
C. Only one of them has diagonals that are perpendicular
D. Only one of them has 4 equal angles

---

211.   *Mathematics Knowledge*

Points A: (1, 6) and B: (2, 12) are plotted on a coordinate plane. What are the coordinates of the midpoint of line AB?

A. (3, 18)
B. (1.5, 9)
C. (1, 12)
D. (2.5, 9)

209. *Mathematics Knowledge*

Answer: C. Trapezoid

A parallelogram has two sets of parallel sides as does a square, a rectangle, and a rhombus. A trapezoid only has one pair of parallel sides.

210. *Mathematics Knowledge*

Answer: D. Only one of them has 4 equal angles

Both a rhombus and a square have 4 equal sides, 2 sets of parallel sides and perpendicular diagonals. Only a square has 4 equal angles.

211. *Mathematics Knowledge*

Answer: B. (1.5, 9)

According to the midpoint formula, the midpoint of the line joining the points (x_1, y_1) and (x_2, y_2) is given by
$$\left(\frac{x_1 + x_2}{2}, \frac{y_1 + y_2}{2} \right).$$

For this problem, the midpoint of line AB =
$$\left(\frac{1+2}{2}, \frac{6+12}{2} \right) = (1.5, 9).$$

212.   *Mathematics Knowledge*

Points A: (3, 5) and B: (6, 9) are plotted on a coordinate plane. What is the distance between them?

A. 3 units
B. 5 units
C. 4 units
D. 25 units

---

213.   *Mathematics Knowledge*

When two parallel lines are cut by a transversal, the following is true of corresponding angles:

A. They are not congruent
B. They are on opposite sides of the transversal
C. They are congruent
D. They are exterior angles

---

214.   *Mathematics Knowledge*

Lines AB and CD are cut by a transversal EFGH. If angle AFG is congruent to angle DGF, we can conclude that lines AB and CD are parallel because

A. Angle AFG and angle DGF are alternate interior angles
B. Angle AFG and angle DGF are alternate exterior angles
C. Angle AFG and angle DGF are corresponding angles
D. Angle AFG and angle DGF are vertical angles

212.

Answer: B. 5 units

According to the distance formula, the distance between points (x_1, y_1) and (x_2, y_2) on a coordinate plane is given by $d = \sqrt{(x_1 - x_2)^2 + (y_1 - y_2)^2}$.

For this problem
$d = \sqrt{(3-6)^2 + (5-9)^2} = \sqrt{(-3)^2 + (-4)^2} = \sqrt{25} = 5$.

213.

Answer: C. They are congruent

When two parallel lines are cut by a transversal, corresponding angles are congruent. They are on the same side of the transversal with one angle within the parallel lines and the other exterior to them.

214.

Answer: A. Angle AFG and angle DGF are alternate interior angles

Since angles AFG and DGF are on opposite sides of the transversal, they are "alternate"; since they are within the two lines AB and CD they are "interior". When two parallel lines are cut by a transversal, the alternate interior angles are equal.

215. *Mathematics Knowledge*

A storage shed is 12 ft long, 8 ft wide and 10 ft high. What is its volume?

A. 800 cubic ft
B. 1200 cubic ft
C. 960 cubic ft
D. 120 cubic ft

---

216. *Mathematics Knowledge*

The perimeter of a rectangular swimming pool is 200 ft. If the pool is 60 ft long, what is its width?

A. 140 ft
B. 40 ft
C. 80 ft
D. 120 ft

---

217. *Mathematics Knowledge*

A lawn is 180 ft long and 130 ft wide. If lawn care costs $0.50 per square yard, what is the cost of maintaining the lawn?

A. $11,700
B. $2,600
C. $1,800
D. $1,300

215.   *Mathematics Knowledge*

Answer: C. 960 cubic ft

The volume of a rectangular prism is given by V = length x width x height. Hence the volume of the storage shed = 12 x 8 x 10 cubic ft = 960 cubic ft.

---

216.   *Mathematics Knowledge*

Answer: B. 40 ft

The perimeter of a rectangle is twice the sum of its length and width.

If the width of the pool is w, then: 2(60 + w) = 200

120 + 2w = 200 (distributing the left side)
2w = 80 (subtracting 120 from both sides)
w = 40 (dividing both sides by 2)

---

217.   *Mathematics Knowledge*

Answer: D. $1,300

The area of the lawn = 180 x 130 sq. ft = 23400 sq. ft.

Since 1 sq. yd = 9 sq. ft, the area of the lawn in square yards = 23400/ 9 = 2600 sq. yds.

The cost of maintaining 2600 sq. yds = 2600 x $0.50 = $1300.

218.   *Mathematics Knowledge*

A school building is 50 ft tall and casts a shadow 30 ft long. At the same time of day, a flagpole in front of the building casts a shadow 45 ft long. How tall is the flagpole?

A. 75 ft
B. 45 ft
C. 80 ft
D. 95 ft

219.   *Mathematics Knowledge*

How many color pencil boxes 10cm x 5cm x 2cm can be packed in a rectangular container 1m x 0.25m x 0.2m?

A. 1000
B. 1500
C. 500
D. 1250

220.   *Mathematics Knowledge*

What is the area of a circle of diameter 5 cm? Assume π =3.14.

5 cm

A. 78.5 sq. cm
B. 15.725 sq. cm
C. 19.625 sq. cm
D. 20.25 sq. cm

218.

Answer: A. 75 ft

The length of the shadow of an object is proportional to its height. Therefore, if the height of the flagpole is x ft,

$$\frac{50}{x} = \frac{30}{45}$$

Cross-multiplying, 30x = 2250

Dividing both sides by 30, x = 75

219.

Answer: C. 500

The volume of each pencil box = 10cm x 5cm x 2cm = 100 cubic cm.

The volume of the container = 100cm x 25cm x 20cm = 50,000 cubic cm.

The number of pencil boxes that can fit into the container = 50,000/100 = 500.

220.

Answer: C. 19.625 sq. cm

Since the diameter of the circle is 5 cm, the radius r = 2.5 cm.

The area of the circle = $\pi r^2 = 3.14 \times (2.5)^2 = 19.625$ sq. cm

221.

A cylinder of radius 2 inches is 5 inches in height. What is its volume? Assume π =3.14.

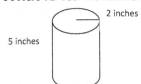

2 inches

5 inches

A. 62.8 sq. in.
B. 15.7 sq. in.
C. 32.4 sq. in.
D. 20.25 sq. in.

222.

What is the volume of a cylinder of diameter 2 ft and height 3.5ft? Assume π =3.14.

A. 43.96 sq. ft
B. 10.99 sq. ft
C. 7.00 sq. ft
D. 22.65 sq. ft.

223.

What is the circumference of a circle of radius 10 cm? Assume π =3.14.

A. 20.0 cm
B. 31.4 cm
C. 6.28 cm
D. 62.8 cm

221. *Mathematics Knowledge*

Answer: A. 62.8 sq. in.

The volume of a cylinder of radius r and height h is given by $V = \pi r^2 h$.

For the given cylinder, $V = 3.14 \times (2)^2 \times 5 = 62.8$ sq. in.

222. *Mathematics Knowledge*

Answer: B. 10.99 sq. ft

The radius of the given cylinder = 1ft.

Since the volume of a cylinder of radius r and height h is $V = \pi r^2 h$, for the given cylinder, V = $3.14 \times (1)^2 \times 3.5 = 10.99$ sq. ft.

223. *Mathematics Knowledge*

Answer: D. 62.8 cm

The circumference of the circle = $2\pi r = 2 \times 3.14 \times 10 = 62.8$ cm.

224.   *Mathematics Knowledge*

The path around a circular park is 2 Km long. Assume π =3.14. The diameter of the park is about:

A. 318 m
B. 521 m
C. 1000 m
D. 637 m

225.   *Mathematics Knowledge*

The radius of a soccer ball is 4.5 inches. What is its volume? Assume π =3.14.

A. 381.5 in^3
B. 1144.5 in^3
C. 254.3 in^3
D. 508.7 in^3

226.   *Mathematics Knowledge*

3/25 is equivalent to:

A. 3/25%
B. 25/3%
C. 8%
D. 12%

224.

Answer: D. 637 m

If the diameter of the park is d, πd = 2 Km, d = 2/3.14 Km = 0.637 Km = 637 m.

225.

Answer: A. 381.5 in³

The volume of a ball of radius r = $\frac{4}{3}\pi r^3$.

The volume of the soccer ball = $\frac{4}{3}(3.14)(4.5)^3$ in³ = 381.5 in³

226.

Answer: D. 12%

To find the percent equivalent of a fraction, multiply the fraction by 100:

(3/25) x 100 = 3 x 4 = 12%

227. *Mathematics Knowledge*

Rina spent 2 hours of her Saturday morning cleaning, 1 hour reading and 2 more hours calling friends. What percent of her morning was spent reading?

A. 5%
B. 25%
C. 18%
D. 20%

228. *Mathematics Knowledge*

A telemarketer called 72 customers in a day. Only 18 of them answered the telephone. What percent of customers was the telemarketer able to talk to?

A. 15%
B. 25%
C. 18%
D. 30%

229. *Mathematics Knowledge*

At the end of February, a winter coat is put on sale for $50.00. If its original price was $75.00, by what percent has the price been reduced?

A. 50%
B. 25%
C. 66.6%
D. 33.3%

227. *Mathematics Knowledge*

Answer: D. 20%

The fraction of time Rina spent reading on Saturday morning is 1/5.

Expressed in percents this is (1/5) x 100 = 100/5 = 20%.

228. *Mathematics Knowledge*

Answer: B. 25%

The fraction of customers the telemarketer spoke to is 18/72 = 1/4.

Expressed in percents this is (1/4) x 100 = 100/4 = 25%.

229. *Mathematics Knowledge*

Answer: D. 33.3%

The price of the coat has been reduced by $25.

The percentage reduction with respect to the original price = (25/75) x 100 = (1/3) x 100 = 33.3%.

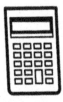

230. *Mathematics Knowledge*

A school has 300 students. 45% of them are boys. How many female students does the school have?

A. 55
B. 135
C. 165
D. 150

231. *Mathematics Knowledge*

A baseball team won 80% of the 15 games they played in a particular season. How many games did they lose?

A. 2
B. 11
C. 3
D. 7

232. *Mathematics Knowledge*

Mr. Morton bought a shirt for $35.50, a pair of pants for $29.00 and a wallet for $25.00. If the sales tax rate is 6%, what was the amount of the total tax on his purchase?

A. $6.00
B. $5.37
C. $5.63
D. $5.50

230. *Mathematics Knowledge*

Answer: C. 165

Since 45% of the students are boys, the percentage of girls is 55%.

Therefore the number of girls is (55/100) x 300 = 55 x 3 = 165.

---

231. *Mathematics Knowledge*

Answer: C. 3

Since the team won 80% of the games, they lost 20% of them.

Therefore, the number of games they lost = (20/100) x 15 = (1/5) x 15 = 3.

---

232. *Mathematics Knowledge*

Answer: B. $5.37

The total amount Mr. Morton spent = $35.50 + $29.00 + $25.00 = $89.50.

6% of $89.50 = (6/100) x $89.50 = $5.37.

233.

In a high school music program of 150 students, 60% are in band. 20% of the band students play the clarinet. How many clarinet players does the school have?

A. 18
B. 30
C. 90
D. 20

234.

In a department store, a pair of socks is normally priced at $5.00. Mrs. Smith buys a pair of socks at the Valentine's Day sale rate of $4.50. Mrs. Brown is a preferred customer and gets a special rate of $4.00 per pair. How many percent more does Mrs. Brown save than Mrs. Smith?

A. 10%
B. 30%
C. 15%
D. 20%

235.

Mark invests $200,000 at an annual interest rate of 6%. If he needs an income of $18,000 from his investment every year, how much additional money should he invest at the same interest rate?

A. $300,000
B. $150,000
C. $200,000
D. $100,000

233. *Mathematics Knowledge*

Answer: A. 18

The number of band students = (60/100) x 150 = (3/5) x 150 = 90.

The number of clarinet players = (20/100) x 90 = (1/5) x 90 = 18.

234. *Mathematics Knowledge*

Answer: A. 10%

Mrs. Smith saves $0.50 which is (0.5/5) x 100 = 10% of the original price.

Mrs. Brown saves $1.00 which is (1/5) x 100 = 20% of the original price.

So Mrs. Brown saves 20% - 10% = 10% more than Mrs. Smith.

235. *Mathematics Knowledge*

Answer: D. $100,000

Mark's annual income from his $200,000 investment = (6/100) x 200,000 = $12,000. He needs $6,000 more every year. If Mark invests y dollars more, then 6% of y must be $6,000:

$$\frac{6}{100} \times y = 6000$$

$$\frac{6y}{100} = 6000$$

$$6y = 600,000$$

$$y = 100,000$$

236. *Mathematics Knowledge*

In a medical clinic, one doctor can see 25 patients a day. The clinic typically gets 500 patients each day. How many doctors must be on staff if the clinic is required to have 10% extra doctors on hand to attend to emergencies?

A. 20
B. 22
C. 25
D. 21

---

237. *Mathematics Knowledge*

All employees of a company will be given an equal share of 15% of the annual profit of $2,000,000. If the company has 50 salaried workers and 25 hourly workers, what is the total amount to be given to the hourly workers?

A. $300,000
B. $150,000
C. $200,000
D. $100,000

---

238. *Mathematics Knowledge*

How many 6 oz candy bars are there in a 3lb package of candy bars?

A. 3
B. 18
C. 6
D. 8

236. *Mathematics Knowledge*

Answer: B. 22

If one doctor can see 25 patients a day, the number of doctors needed to see 500 patients is 500/25 = 20.

The number of extra doctors needed on staff is 10% of 20 = (10/100) x 20 = 2.

Therefore the total number of doctors the clinic needs = 20 + 2 = 22.

237. *Mathematics Knowledge*

Answer: D. $100,000

The amount of profit to be shared is 15% of $2,000,000 = (15/100) x $2,000,000 = $300,000.

Since there are 75 employees, the share of each employee = $300,000/75 = $4,000.

The total amount to be given to the hourly workers = $4,000 x 25 = $100,000.

238. *Mathematics Knowledge*

Answer: D. 8

Since 1 lb = 16 oz, 3lb = 48 oz.

Hence there are 48/6 = 8 candy bars in a 3 lb package.

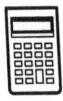

239. *Mathematics Knowledge*

Apples are sold at $1.28 per pound. If an average apple weighs 5 oz, the cost of 6 apples is about:

A. $2.00
B. $3.20
C. $2.40
D. $3.60

240. *Mathematics Knowledge*

The average height of the 4 children in the Smith family is 50 inches. Sara is 54 inches tall, Andy is 52 inches tall, Roger is 49 inches tall. How tall is Madison?

A. 45 inches
B. 46 inches
C. 44 inches
D. 42 inches

241. *Mathematics Knowledge*

A baker buys 50 lbs of flour on Monday, 46 lbs on Tuesday and 57 lbs on Wednesday. What is the average amount of flour he bought each day?

A. 50 lbs
B. 46 lbs
C. 51 lbs
D. 52 lbs

239.

Answer: C. $2.40

Since 1 lb = 16 oz, the cost of 1 apple = $1.28 x (5/16) = $0.40.

Hence the cost of 6 apples = 6 x 0.40 = $2.40

240.

Answer: A. 45 inches

Since the average height of the 4 children is 50 inches, their total height is 50 x 4 = 200 inches.

The sum of the heights of Sara, Andy and Roger is 54 + 52 + 49 = 155 inches.

Hence Madison's height is 200 – 155 = 45 inches.

241.

Answer: C. 51 lbs

The average amount of flour the baker bought each day = (50 + 46 + 57)/3 = 153/3 = 51 lbs.

242.

Mathematics Knowledge

A car can drive 350 miles on 15 gallons of gas. The driver starts out on a 1500 mile trip with a full tank of gas. How many times must she refill the gas tank on the way?

A. 2
B. 3
C. 4
D. 1

243.

Mathematics Knowledge

An office building normally uses 35 gallons of drinking water a day. During their annual conference, the usage goes up to 50 gallons a day. If the annual conference was held from 4th to 7th March (both days included), how many gallons of drinking water did they use during the month of March?

A. 1145 gallons
B. 1085 gallons
C. 1550 gallons
D. 1130 gallons

244.

Mathematics Knowledge

Mrs. Morris insured her jewellery for $150,000. If the annual premium is $0.50 per $100 of insurance, how much premium does she pay every quarter?

A. $750
B. $187.50
C. $375
D. $1875.00

242. *Mathematics Knowledge*

Answer: C. 4

The gas tank must be refilled at least every 350 miles: after 350 miles, 700 miles, 1050 miles and 1400 miles.

243. *Mathematics Knowledge*

Answer: A. 1145 gallons

Drinking water use during the 4 days of the conference = 4 x 50 = 200 gallons.

Drinking water use for the remaining 27 days in March = 27 x 35 = 945 gallons.

Total drinking water use in March = 200 + 945 = 1145 gallons.

244. *Mathematics Knowledge*

Answer: B. $187.50

The premium for the whole year = 150,000 x (0.5/100) = $750.

The premium for each quarter = $750/4 = $187.50.

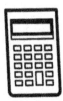

245. *Mathematics Knowledge*

Sara can buy a garden tiller for $185 or rent one for $15 a day. It will be cheaper to buy the tiller if Sara:

A. Uses the tiller 5 times a year for 3 years
B. Uses the tiller 3 times a year for 4 years
C. Uses the tiller 5 times a year for 2 years
D. Uses the tiller 2 times a year for 5 years

---

246. *Mathematics Knowledge*

Scott can mow a lawn in 2 hours. Mike can mow the same lawn in 3 hours. If they work together, how long will it take them to mow the lawn?

A. 50 minutes
B. 36 minutes
C. 1 hour 12 minutes
D. 1 hour 40 minutes

---

247. *Mathematics Knowledge*

Nick's brother is 2 years older than him. If the sum of their ages is 26, how old is Nick?

A. 24
B. 13
C. 11
D. 12

245.

Answer: A. Uses the tiller 5 times a year for 3 years

Since $\dfrac{185}{15} = 12\dfrac{1}{3}$, it will be cheaper to buy a tiller only if Sara uses it more than 12 times.

246.

Answer: C. 1 hour 12 minutes

In 1 hour Scott can mow $\dfrac{1}{2}$ of the lawn. In 1 hour Mike can mow $\dfrac{1}{3}$ of the lawn.

Together, in 1 hour they can mow $\dfrac{1}{2} + \dfrac{1}{3} = \dfrac{5}{6}$ of the lawn. So, they can mow the whole lawn in $\dfrac{6}{5}$ hours = 1 hour 12 minutes.

247.

Answer: D. 12

Since Nick's brother is 2 years older than him, the sum of their ages is 2 more than twice Nick's age.

So, twice Nick's age is 24 and Nick's age is 12.

248. *Mathematics Knowledge*

A box contains 6 blue marbles, 3 red marbles and 11 white marbles. If you pick one marble from the box at random without looking, what is the probability that you will pick a blue marble?

A. 3/7
B. 3/10
C. 1/2
D. 7/10

---

249. *Mathematics Knowledge*

Maria has 6 pairs of pants, 10 shirts, and 4 scarves to choose from. How many different combinations of outfits can she create from her wardrobe?

A. 20
B. 240
C. 4
D. 60

---

250. *Mathematics Knowledge*

In how many ways can you arrange 5 books on a shelf?

A. 120
B. 240
C. 30
D. 60

248.   *Mathematics Knowledge*

Answer: B. 3/10

Since the total number of marbles is 20, the probability of picking a blue marble from the box at random = 6/20 = 3/10.

---

249.   *Mathematics Knowledge*

Answer: B. 240

Assuming any skirt can be matched with any pair of pants and any scarf, the number of possible combinations is 6 x 10 x 4 = 240.

---

250.   *Mathematics Knowledge*

Answer: A. 120

Since there are 5 books, the first position on the shelf can be filled in 5 ways. Once the first book is in place, the second position can be filled in 4 ways by one of the 4 remaining books. Similarly, the third position can be filled in 3 ways, the fourth position in 2 ways and the fifth position in 1 way. Hence the number of ways in which the books can be arranged on the shelf = 5 x 4 x 3 x 2 x 1 = 120.

251.   *General Science*

What does DNA stand for?

A. Defined nucleus architecture
B. Differential nucleic acid
C. Deoxyribonucleic acid
D. Dehydrogenated nucleic acid

252.   *General Science*

**Which type of cell contains hemoglobin, a molecule
that transports oxygen in human blood?**

A. White blood cells
B. Red blood cells
C. Platelets
D. Epidermal cells

253.   *General Science*

The role of the endocrine system is to:

A. Release chemical signals into the body to regulate
   various bodily functions
B. Carry oxygenated blood and nutrients to all cells of the
   body
C. Send out automated or reflexive motor commands in
   response to stimuli
D. Defend the body against foreign invaders

251. *General Science*

Answer: C. Deoxyribonucleic acid

DNA is a nucleic acid (deoxyribonucleic acid) that carries the code for the amino acid sequence of proteins and the instructions for its own replication. It is made of 2 long strands of nucleotides linked in a double helix (shaped like a twisted ladder). The sequence of nucleotides determines the individual hereditary characteristics that are transmitted from parents to offspring.

252. *General Science*

Answer: B. Red blood cells

There are two classes of cells in blood, red blood cells and white blood cells. Red blood cells are the most numerous and contain hemoglobin, which carries oxygen. White blood cells are larger than red blood cells and have the ability to engulf invaders to help protect the body from infection and disease. White blood cells are not confined to the blood vessels and can enter the interstitial fluid between cells.

253. *General Science*

Answer: A. Release chemical signals into the body to regulate various bodily functions

The function of the endocrine system is to manufacture proteins called hormones. Hormones are released into the bloodstream and are carried to a target tissue where they stimulate an action. Hormones are specific and fit receptors on the cell surface of the target tissue (i.e., specific hormones bind with specific target tissues). Receptor binding then activates an enzyme which creates a "second messenger", another compound that travels from the cell membrane to the nucleus. The second messenger triggers the genes found in the nucleus to turn on or turn off a specific response.

254. *General Science*

What is the function of an enzyme?

A. To speed up a chemical reaction
B. To provide energy to a chemical reaction
C. To increase the volume of the substrate
D. To digest the waste material of a chemical reaction

255. *General Science*

The main source of glucose in the human diet is/are:

A. Carbohydrates
B. Fat
C. Protein
D. Most forms of food

256. *General Science*

What is the difference between someone's genotype and phenotype?

A. Everyone has a genotype but not everyone has a phenotype
B. Genotype refers to genetic makeup and phenotype refers to the traits or characteristics that result from that makeup
C. Genotypes are observable and phenotypes are rarely observable
D. Phenotype refers to genetic makeup and genotype refers to the traits or characteristics that result from that makeup

254.

Answer: A. To speed up a chemical reaction

The function of an enzyme is to speed up a chemical reaction by lowering the amount of energy required for it to occur. Enzymes are biological catalysts (proteins) that are not consumed by the reaction and so are available to catalyze more reactions.

255.

Answer: A. Carbohydrates

Carbohydrates are the main source of energy (glucose) in the human diet. The two types of carbohydrates are simple and complex. Complex carbohydrates have greater nutritional value because they take longer to digest, contain dietary fiber, and do not excessively elevate blood sugar levels. Common sources of carbohydrates are fruits, vegetables, grains, dairy products, and legumes.

256.

Answer: B. Genotype refers to genetic makeup and phenotype refers to the traits or characteristics that result from that makeup

A genotype is an organism's actual genetic makeup. It refers to the inherited genetic instructions contained within its DNA. A phenotype is any observable trait or characteristic that results from this genetic makeup, i.e., it is the observable expression of the genotype.

257. *General Science*

The scientific name for humans is *Homo sapiens*.
This refers to our:

A. Genus and species
B. Kingdom and phylum
C. Class and order
D. Phylum and class

---

258. *General Science*

The _____ carries oxygenated blood and
nutrients to all cells of the body and returns carbon
dioxide waste to be expelled from the lungs.

A. nervous system
B. circulatory system
C. excretory system
D. endocrine system

---

259. *General Science*

The amount of glucose in the blood (blood sugar
levels) is regulated by which of the following?

A. Testosterone in males and estrogen in females
B. Adrenaline and glucose
C. Adrenaline and insulin
D. Insulin and estrogen

257.

Answer: A. Genus and species

Biology uses a system of taxonomy to classify species. The order of classification for humans is as follows: <u>Kingdom</u>: Animalia; <u>Phylum</u>: Chordata; <u>Subphylum</u>: Vertebrata; <u>Class</u>: Mammalia; <u>Order</u>: Primate; <u>Family</u>: Hominadae; <u>Genus</u>: Homo; <u>Species</u>: sapiens.

258.

Answer: B. circulatory system

Unoxygenated blood enters the right atrium of the heart through the inferior and superior vena cava. The blood flows through the tricuspid valve to the right ventricle to the pulmonary arteries and then to the lungs where it is oxygenated. It returns to the heart through the pulmonary vein into the left atrium, travels through the bicuspid valve to the left ventricle from where it is pumped to all parts of the body through the aorta.

259.

Answer: C. Adrenaline and insulin

Adrenaline and insulin regulate the concentration of glucose in the blood. Adrenaline is produced by the adrenal medulla and insulin is produced by the pancreas.

260. *General Science*

What is the function of antibodies?

A. To regulate hormone levels
B. To protect the body from viruses, toxins, and bacteria
C. To assist with digestive processes
D. To stimulate nerve activity in the brain

261. *General Science*

Which sex chromosomes are found in males?

A. XX
B. AB
C. XY
D. YY

262. *General Science*

Fertilization in humans usually occurs in the:

A. Cervix
B. Ovary
C. Fallopian tubes
D. Vagina

260. *General Science*

Answer: B. To protect the body from viruses, toxins, and bacteria

Antibodies are part of the immune system. They identify and neutralize foreign objects in the body such as viruses, toxins, and bacteria. Antibodies are Y-shaped proteins that bind with the antigen (the foreign object) at the top ends of their Y-shape. This "tags" the antigen for attack by the immune system or blocks key parts of the antigen making it unable to invade or survive.

261. *General Science*

Answer: C. XY

Humans have 23 pairs of chromosomes (for a total of 46 chromosomes). Of these, 22 pairs are called autosomes and contain the genetic hereditary information. 1 pair is called sex chromosomes and determines gender. Males have an XY pair of sex chromosomes and females have an XX pair. In the creation of life, the female contributes an X chromosome and the male contributes either an X or a Y chromosome. The sex chromosome contributed by the male's sperm determines the gender of the fetus.

262. *General Science*

Answer: C. Fallopian tubes

Fertilization of the egg by the sperm normally occurs in the fallopian tube. The fertilized egg then implants in the uterine lining for development.

263. *General Science*

A cell containing a cell wall and chloroplasts is which type of cell?

A. A plant cell
B. An animal cell
C. A stem cell
D. A brain cell

---

264. *General Science*

Humans have how many pairs of chromosomes?

A. 46
B. 12
C. 44
D. 23

---

265. *General Science*

Identify the correct sequence of organization of living things from lower to higher order:

A. Cell, organelle, organ, tissue, system, organism
B. Cell, tissue, organ, organelle, system, organism
C. Organelle, cell, tissue, organ, system, organism
D. Organelle, tissue, cell, organ, system, organism

263.

Answer: A. A plant cell

Plant cells differ from animal cells in that they have a cell wall and chloroplasts. Cell walls are made mostly of cellulose and are thick enough to provide support and protection, yet porous enough to allow water and dissolved substances to enter. Chloroplasts contain chlorophyll, a pigment involved in photosynthesis that is capable of trapping sunlight.

264.

Answer: D. 23

Humans have 23 pairs of chromosomes (46 chromosomes total). Chromosomes consist of chromatin, which are complexes of DNA and proteins. Chromosomal DNA carries the majority of an organism's genetic material. A specialized subunit of the cell called the mitochondria also has some DNA-containing genes. Mitochondrial DNA is often called maternal because offspring receive their mitochondrial DNA from their mother.

265.

Answer: C. Organelle, cell, tissue, organ, system, organism

Organelles are parts of cells. They are specialized subunits within cells that perform specific functions. Cells make up tissues and tissues make up organs. Organs work together in systems (for example, the respiratory system or the digestive system) and an organism is the whole living creature.

266.   *General Science*

Proteins are made up of:

A. Carbohydrates
B. Amino acids
C. Lipids
D. Fatty acids

---

267.   *General Science*

Why are viruses considered 'obligate' parasites?

A. Because once they enter the host, they are obligated to infect it
B. Because the immune system of the host is obligated to combat the virus
C. Because they are not reliant on the host for any of the means of their own survival or reproduction
D. Because they rely on the host for their own reproduction

---

268.   *General Science*

The blood vessels in the circulatory system are:

A. Lymph capillaries and lymph nodes
B. Arteries, veins, and epidermis
C. Arteries, capillaries, and veins
D. Capillaries and platelets

266. *General Science*

Answer: B. Amino acids

Amino acids are the building blocks of proteins. The primary structure of a protein is determined by the linear sequence of amino acids in the protein. Proteins are important compounds that are involved in nearly every cellular process. Since not every amino acid can be synthesized (made) by the body, we have to obtain the essential amino acids from food. Digesting protein breaks the proteins up into free amino acids that are available to the body for creating new proteins.

267. *General Science*

Answer: D. Because they rely on the host for their own reproduction

Although viruses are not classified as living things, they greatly affect other living things by disrupting cell activity. They are considered to be obligate parasites because they rely on the host for their own reproduction.

268. *General Science*

Answer: C. Arteries, capillaries, and veins

There are three kinds of blood vessels in the circulatory system: arteries, capillaries, and veins. Arteries carry oxygenated blood away from the heart to organs in the body. Arteries branch off to form smaller arterioles in organs. Arterioles form tiny capillaries that reach every tissue. Downstream, capillaries combine to form larger venules. Venules combine to form larger veins that return blood to the heart. Arteries and veins differ in the direction they carry blood.

269. *General Science*

A ball rolls down a smooth hill. Ignoring the effects of air resistance, which of the following is a true statement?

A. The ball has more energy at the start of its descent than just before it hits the bottom of the hill, because it is higher up at the beginning
B. The ball has less energy at the start of its descent than just before it hits the bottom of the hill, because it is moving more quickly at the end
C. The ball has the same energy throughout its descent, because positional energy is converted to energy of motion
D. The ball has the same energy throughout its descent, because a single object cannot gain or lose energy

---

270. *General Science*

A boulder sitting on the edge of a cliff has which type of energy?

A. Kinetic energy
B. Latent energy
C. No energy
D. Potential energy

---

271. *General Science*

Which statement is the most accurate?

A. Mass is always constant; weight can change by location
B. Mass and weight are both always constant
C. Weight is always constant; mass can change by location
D. Mass and weight can both change by location

269. *General Science*

Answer: C. The ball has the same energy throughout its descent, because positional energy is converted to energy of motion

The principle of Conservation of Energy states that energy is neither created nor destroyed, but may be transformed. It is true that the ball has more potential energy when it is higher, and that it has more kinetic energy when it is moving quickly at the bottom of its descent. However, the total sum of all kinds of energy in the ball remains constant, if we neglect losses to heat/friction.

270. *General Science*

Answer: D. Potential energy

The boulder would have kinetic energy if it fell off the cliff and started falling. Sitting on the edge of the cliff, the boulder possesses potential energy that is imparted from the force of gravity. Potential energy is the energy stored in a system based on its position or condition, rather than motion.

271. *General Science*

Answer: A. Mass is always constant; weight can change by location

Mass is a measure of the amount of matter in an object and doesn't change with location. Two objects of equal mass will balance each other on a simple balance scale no matter where the scale is located. Weight is the measure of the Earth's pull of gravity on an object and can change depending on changes in the gravitational field. An object on Earth will feel heavier than on the Moon because of the gravitation pull of the Earth. Two objects of equal mass will have different weights on the Earth and the Moon.

272. *General Science*

Sound can be transmitted in all of the following except:

A. Air
B. Water
C. Diamond
D. A vacuum

273. *General Science*

How does a steam radiator deliver heat energy to a room?

A. Radiation
B. Conduction
C. Convection
D. Contact

274. *General Science*

The Doppler Effect is associated most closely with which property of waves?

A. Amplitude
B. Wavelength
C. Frequency
D. Intensity

272.　　　　　　　　　　　　　　*General Science*

Answer: D. A vacuum

Sound, a longitudinal wave, is transmitted by vibrations of molecules. It can be transmitted through any gas, liquid, or solid. However, it cannot be transmitted through a vacuum because there are no particles present to vibrate and propagate the wave to adjacent particles.

273.　　　　　　　　　　　　　　*General Science*

Answer: C. Convection

The air near the radiator gets hot, expands, and rises. New cooler air replaces the hot, rising air. This convection cycle repeats over and over until the room reaches a higher temperature.

274.　　　　　　　　　　　　　　*General Science*

Answer: C. Frequency

The Doppler Effect accounts for an apparent increase in frequency when a wave source moves toward a wave receiver or apparent decrease in frequency when a wave source moves away from a wave receiver. (Note that the receiver could also be moving toward or away from the source.) As the wave fronts are released, motion toward the receiver mimics more frequent wave fronts, while motion away from the receiver mimics less frequent wave fronts.

275. *General Science*

Sonar works by _____ .

A. timing how long it takes sound to reach a certain speed
B. bouncing sound waves between two metal plates
C. bouncing sound waves off an object and timing how long it takes for the sound to return
D. evaluating the motion and amplitude of sound

276. *General Science*

A converging lens produces a real image _____.

A. never
B. when the object is exactly at a distance of one focal length
C. when the object is within one focal length of the lens
D. when the object is further than one focal length from the lens

277. *General Science*

Under a microscope with 440X magnification, an object with a diameter of 0.1 millimeters appears to have a diameter of _____.

A. 4.4 millimeters
B. 44 millimeters
C. 440 millimeters
D. 4400 millimeters

275.   *General Science*

Answer: C. bouncing sound waves off an object and timing how long it takes for the sound to return

Sonar is used to measure distances. Sound waves are sent out, and the time is measured for the sound to hit an obstacle and bounce back. By using the known speed of sound, observers (or machines) can calculate the distance to the obstacle.

276.   *General Science*

Answer: D. when the object is further than one focal length from the lens

A converging lens produces real images when the object is further than one focal length from the lens. Rays of light bounce off the object, hit the lens, and are focused on the other side of the lens producing a real image. When the object is closer than one focal length from the lens, rays of light do not converge on the other side; they diverge.

277.   *General Science*

Answer: B. 44 millimeters

To calculate the magnified dimensions of an object, multiply the actual dimensions by the magnification power of the instrument. For this example: (0.1 millimeter diameter) x (440) = 44 millimeter.

278.   *General Science*

Which of the following statements is NOT true?

A. Heat cannot pass spontaneously from a colder object to a hotter object
B. Systems that are nearly always in a state of equilibrium are called reversible systems
C. Some machines (called perfect machines) can absorb heat from a heat source and do an equal amount of work without losing any heat to the environment
D. Work occurs when heat is transferred from hotter objects to cooler objects

---

279.   *General Science*

Which of the following are true of electrically charged objects?

A. Like charges repel one another
B. Opposite charges attract each other
C. A neutral object has no net change
D. All of the above

---

280.   *General Science*

Which of the following is a correct explanation for astronaut 'weightlessness'?

A. Astronauts in space are so far from planets that the effects of gravity are small
B. Astronauts in space feel the effects of gravity, but it is diminished by the powerful thrust of the spacecraft engines
C. Astronauts do not feel the pull of gravity in space because space is a vacuum
D. Astronauts do not feel the pull of gravity in space because of black holes

278. *General Science*

Answer: C. Some machines (called perfect machines) can absorb heat from a heat source and do an equal amount of work without losing any heat to the environment

The first part of the second law of thermodynamics tells us that no machine is 100% efficient. It is impossible to construct a machine that absorbs heat from a heat source and performs an equal amount of work because some heat will always be lost to the environment.

279. *General Science*

Answer: D. All of the above

Electrically charged objects share all of these characteristics. A positive charge repels a positive charge and a negative charge repels a negative charge. A positive charge and a negative charge will attract each other. A neutral object has no net charge, meaning that its overall charge is neither positive nor negative.

280. *General Science*

Answer: A. Astronauts in space are so far from planets that the effects of gravity are small

Gravitational force is inversely proportional to distance squared from a massive body. This means that the larger the distance over which gravity has to act, the smaller its effect. When an astronaut is in space, s/he is far enough from the center of mass of any planet that the gravitational force is very small, and s/he feels 'weightless'.

281.

The Law of Conservation of Energy states that:

A. Reactions cannot occur without the aid of catalysts
B. Objects always fall toward large masses such as planets
C. Energy is neither created nor destroyed, but may change form
D. Natural resources will be depleted if not managed properly

282.

The electromagnetic radiation with the longest wave length is/are _____ .

A. radio waves
B. red light
C. X-rays
D. ultraviolet light

283.

As a train approaches, the whistle sounds

A. Higher, because it has a higher apparent frequency
B. Lower, because it has a lower apparent frequency
C. Higher, because it has a lower apparent frequency
D. Lower, because it has a higher apparent frequency

281.

Answer: C. Energy is neither created nor destroyed, but may change form

Energy can be transformed into various forms such as kinetic energy, potential energy, electric energy, or heat energy, but the total amount of energy remains constant.

282.

Answer: A. radio waves

Radio waves have longer wave lengths than visible light, which in turn has longer wave lengths than ultraviolet or X-ray radiation. Wave length is inversely proportional to frequency. This means that the longer the wavelength, the lower the frequency and vice versa. Since radio waves are considered much less harmful than ultraviolet or X-ray radiation, you can infer that they are less energetic, i.e., have a lower frequency and longer wavelength.

283.

Answer: A. Higher, because it has a higher apparent frequency

By the Doppler Effect, when a source of sound is moving toward an observer, the wave fronts are released closer together, i.e., with a greater apparent frequency. Higher frequency sounds are higher in pitch.

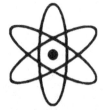

284. *General Science*

Resistance is measured in units called:

A. Watts
B. Volts
C. Ohms
D. Current

285. *General Science*

A 10 ohm resistor and a 50 ohm resistor are connected in parallel. If the current in the 10 ohm resistor is 5 amperes, the current (in amperes) running through the 50 ohm resistor is _____.

A. 1
B. 50
C. 25
D. 60

286. *General Science*

A light bulb is connected in series with a rotating coil within a magnetic field. The brightness of the light may be increased by any of the following except:

A. Rotating the coil more rapidly
B. Adding more loops to the coil
C. Using tighter loops for the coil
D. Using a stronger magnetic field

284.

General Science

Answer: C. Ohms

A watt is a unit of energy. Potential difference is measured in a unit called the volt. Current is the number of electrons per second that flow past a point in a circuit. An ohm is the unit for resistance. Resistance is the ability of material to oppose the flow of electrons through it.

285.

General Science

Answer: A. 1

Ohm's Law defines the relationship between voltage (V), current (I), and resistance (R):
V = IR (or I = V/R or R = V/I)

In a parallel circuit, the voltage is the same across the branches. Use Ohm's Law and the information known about the 10 ohm resistor to calculate the voltage: V = (5 amperes) (10 ohms) = 50 volts

Use Ohm's Law again to calculate the current running through the 50 ohm resistor. I = (50 volts) ÷ (50 ohms) = 1 ampere.

286.

General Science

Answer: C. Using tighter loops for the coil

A rotating coil in a magnetic field generates electric current. Faraday's Law states that the amount of electromagnetic force generated is proportional to the rate of change of magnetic flux through the loop. This increases if the coil is rotated more rapidly (A), if there are more loops (B), or if the magnetic field is stronger (D). Tighter loops would not change the amount of material in the loops.

287.   *General Science*

According to the Ideal Gas Law, if the volume of a confined gas is increased, what happens to the pressure? Assume that the temperature and number of gas molecules remains constant.

A. The pressure increases
B. The pressure decreases
C. The pressure stays the same
D. There is not enough information given to answer this question

288.   *General Science*

Surface ocean currents are caused by which of the following?

A. Temperature
B. Changes in density of water
C. Wind
D. Tidal forces

289.   *General Science*

What is a large, rotating, low-pressure system accompanied by heavy precipitation and strong winds known as?

A. A hurricane
B. A tornado
C. A thunderstorm
D. A tsunami

287. *General Science*

Answer: B. The pressure decreases

The Ideal Gas Law defines the relationship between pressure (P), volume (V), and temperature (T) in an ideal gas:
$PV = nRT$, where n is the number of moles (a quantity) of gas and R is a constant

Rearranging the equation for volume gives: $V = nRT/P$. Because the temperature and number of gas molecules remains constant, everything on the right side of the equation remains constant except for P, which is inversely proportional to V. An increase in volume will give a decrease in pressure and vice versa.

288. *General Science*

Answer: C. Wind

A current is a large mass of continuously moving oceanic water. Surface ocean currents are mainly wind-driven and occur in all of the world's oceans (example: the Gulf Stream). This is in contrast to deep ocean currents, which are driven by changes in density.

289. *General Science*

Answer A. A hurricane

Hurricanes are storms that develop when warm, moist air carried by trade winds rotates around a low-pressure eye. These form a large, rotating, low-pressure system and are accompanied by heavy precipitation and strong winds. They are also known as tropical cyclones or typhoons.

290. *General Science*

What are the most significant and abundant elements in the biosphere?

A. Carbon, hydrogen, oxygen, nitrogen, phosphorus
B. Carbon, hydrogen, sodium, iron, calcium
C. Carbon, oxygen, sulfur, manganese, iron
D. Carbon, hydrogen, oxygen, nickel, sodium, nitrogen

291. *General Science*

Which of the following is the longest (largest) unit of geological time?

A. Solar year
B. Epoch
C. Period
D. Era

292. *General Science*

The salinity of ocean water is closest to
_____ .

A. 0.035 %
B. 0.35 %
C. 3.5 %
D. 35 %

290. *General Science*

Answer: A. Carbon, hydrogen, oxygen, nitrogen, phosphorus

Organic matter (and life as we know it) is based on carbon atoms, bonded to hydrogen and oxygen. Nitrogen and phosphorus are the next most significant elements, followed by sulfur and then trace nutrients such as iron, sodium, calcium, and others.

291. *General Science*

Answer: D. Era

Geological time is measured by many units, but the longest unit listed here (and indeed the longest used to describe the biological development of the planet) is the Era. Eras are subdivided into Periods, which are further divided into Epochs.

292. *General Science*

Answer: C. 3.5 %

Salinity, or concentration of dissolved salt, can be measured in mass ratio (i.e., mass of salt divided by mass of sea water). For Earth's oceans, the salinity is approximately 3.5 %, or 35 parts per thousand. Note that answers (A) and (D) can be eliminated, because (A) is so dilute as to be hardly saline, while (D) is so concentrated that it would not support ocean life.

293. *General Science*

Members of the same animal species _____.

A. look identical
B. never adapt differently
C. are able to reproduce with each other
D. are found in the same geographic location

294. *General Science*

In which layer of the atmosphere would you expect most weather conditions to occur?

A. Troposphere
B. Thermosphere
C. Mesosphere
D. Stratosphere

295. *General Science*

Which is the correct order for the layers of Earth's atmosphere?

A. Troposphere, stratosphere, mesosphere, and thermosphere
B. Mesosphere, stratosphere, troposphere, and thermosphere
C. Troposphere, stratosphere, thermosphere, and mesosphere
D. Thermosphere, troposphere, stratosphere, mesosphere

293.

General Science

Answer: C. are able to reproduce with each other

Although members of the same animal species may look alike, adapt alike, or be found near each other, the only requirement is that they be able to reproduce with one another. This ability to reproduce within the group is considered the hallmark of a species.

294.

General Science

Answer: A. Troposphere

The troposphere is the lowest portion of the Earth's atmosphere. It contains the highest amount of water and aerosol. Because it touches the Earth's surface features, friction builds. For all of these reasons, weather is most likely to occur in the troposphere.

295.

General Science

Answer: A. Troposphere, stratosphere, mesosphere, and thermosphere

The troposphere is the layer closest to the Earth and is where all weather occurs. There are few clouds in the stratosphere, but weather balloons can float in this region. Air temperatures start to drop in the mesosphere. The coldest spot on Earth is where the mesosphere meets the thermosphere. The thermosphere extends into outer space.

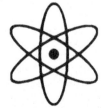

296.

The Moon orbits the Earth every _____ days.

A. 7
B. 27
C. 30
D. 365

297.

Earth is the ___ planet away from the Sun in our solar system.

A. fifth
B. fourth
C. third
D. sixth

298.

The Earth's atmosphere is composed mainly of which of the following?

A. Oxygen and nitrogen
B. Carbon and hydrogen
C. Carbon and oxygen
D. Nitrogen and carbon

296.

Answer: B. 27

The Moon circles the Earth every 27 days. The Earth circles the Sun every 365 days. The relative position of the Earth, Moon, and Sun is responsible for our perception of the phases of the Moon, known as lunar phases.

297.

Answer: C. third

Earth is the third planet away from the Sun in our solar system. The order of the planets, based on distance from the Sun (closest to farthest) is: Mercury, Venus, Earth, Mars, Jupiter, Saturn, Uranus, and Neptune (Pluto is no longer classified as a planet). An easy way to remember this is to use the phrase "**M**y **V**ery **E**ducated **M**other **J**ust **S**aw **U**ncle **N**ick", with the first letter of each word representing a planet.

298.

Answer: A. Oxygen and nitrogen

The atmosphere is composed mainly of oxygen and nitrogen. Earth is the only planet that is known to support life.

299.   *General Science*

If the niches of two species overlap, what usually results?

A. A symbiotic relationship
B. Cooperation
C. Competition
D. A new species

---

300.   *General Science*

A clownfish is protected by the sea anemone's tentacles. In turn, the anemone receives uneaten food from the clownfish. This is an example of:

A. Mutualism
B. Parasitism
C. Commensalism
D. Competition

---

301.   *General Science*

How many oceans are there on Earth?

A. 5
B. 4
C. 3
D. 6

299. *General Science*

Answer: C. Competition

A niche is the relative position of a species or population within an ecosystem. Two species that occupy the same habitat or eat the same food are said to be in competition with one another.

300. *General Science*

Answer: A. Mutualism

Neither the clownfish nor the anemone cause harmful effects towards one another and both benefit from their relationship. Mutualism is when two species that occupy a similar space benefit from their relationship.

301. *General Science*

Answer: A. 5

An ocean is a major body of saline water. Approximately 71% percent of the Earth is covered by oceans. The oceans are: the Pacific, Atlantic, Indian, Antarctic, and Arctic oceans.

302.   *General Science*

Which of the following types of rock are made from magma?

A. Fossils
B. Sedimentary
C. Metamorphic
D. Igneous

---

303.   *General Science*

_____ are cracks in the plates of the earth's crust, along which the plates move.

A. Faults
B. Ridges
C. Earthquakes
D. Volcanoes

---

304.   *General Science*

Which biome is the most prevalent on Earth?

A. Marine
B. Desert
C. Savanna
D. Tundra

302.

Answer: D. Igneous

Igneous rocks are formed from magma (molten lava). Metamorphic rocks are formed by high temperatures and great pressures. Sedimentary rocks are formed in a process called lithification, in which fluid sediments are transformed into solid sedimentary rock.

303.

Answer: A. Faults

Faults are cracks in the earth's crust. Rapid movement of these faults releases energy that leads to earthquakes. Faults may lead to mismatched edges of ground, forming ridges.

304.

Answer: A. Marine

A biome is a zone of interrelated plant and animal populations as determined by the climate. The marine biome covers 75% of the Earth and is organized based on the depth of water. The littoral zone is from the water's edge to the open sea. It includes coral reef habitats and is the most densely populated area of the marine biome.

305.   *General Science*

The oxygen created during photosynthesis comes
from the breakdown of:

A. Carbon dioxide
B. Water
C. Glucose
D. Carbon monoxide

---

306.   *General Science*

What is the smallest particle that has all of the
properties of an element?

A. Atom
B. Electron
C. Proton
D. Molecule

---

307.   *General Science*

Sodium chloride (NaCl) is an example of a(n):

A. Nonpolar covalent bond
B. Polar covalent bond
C. Ionic bond
D. Hydrogen bond

305.   *General Science*

Answer: B. Water

The formula for photosynthesis is:
$CO_2 + H_2O +$ energy from sunlight $\rightarrow C_6H_{12}O_6 + O_2$

carbon dioxide + water + sunlight $\rightarrow$ glucose + oxygen

In photosynthesis, water is split into hydrogen and oxygen. Oxygen is released as a waste product as carbon dioxide is reduced to sugar (glucose). This requires the input of energy, which comes from the sunlight.

---

306.   *General Science*

Answer: A. Atom

An atom is the smallest particle that has all of the properties of an element. Electrons, protons, and neutrons are particles found within an atom. Electrons are negatively charged particles, protons are positively charged particles, and neutrons are neutral and have no charge. Molecules are compounds made up of two or more atoms.

---

307.   *General Science*

Answer: C. Ionic bond

An ionic bond is formed by the transfer of electrons from metal atoms to nonmetal atoms. Before chlorine and sodium bind, sodium has one valence (binding) electron and chlorine has seven. In order to reach a filled valence shell of eight electrons, sodium gives its one valence electron to chlorine. The atoms now become ions–atoms with an unequal number of protons and electrons. To determine whether the ion is positive or negative, compare the number of protons (+ charge) to the electrons (- charge). If there are more electrons, the ion will be negative.

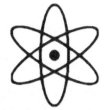

308. *General Science*

What is necessary for diffusion to occur?

A. Carrier proteins
B. Energy
C. A concentration gradient
D. A membrane

---

309. *General Science*

Which of the following will not change in a chemical reaction?

A. Number of moles of products
B. Atomic number of one of the reactants
C. Mass (in grams) of one of the reactants
D. Rate of reaction

---

310. *General Science*

Which reaction below is a decomposition reaction?

A. $HCl + NaOH \rightarrow NaCl + H_2O$
B. $C + O_2 \rightarrow CO_2$
C. $2H_2O \rightarrow 2H_2 + O_2$
D. $CuSO_4 + Fe \rightarrow FeSO_4 + Cu$

308. *General Science*

Answer: C. A concentration gradient

Diffusion is the ability of molecules to move from areas of high concentration to areas of low concentration (a concentration gradient).

---

309. *General Science*

Answer: B. Atomic number of one of the reactants

The atomic number of an element is the number of protons it has and determines which element it is (different elements have different atomic numbers). Atomic number is constant unless an element is involved in a nuclear reaction. Amounts (measured in moles or in grams) of reactants and products do change over the course of a chemical reaction and the rate of a chemical reaction may change due to internal or external processes.

---

310. *General Science*

Answer: C. $2H_2O \rightarrow 2H_2 + O_2$

A decomposition reaction is one in which there are fewer reactants (on the left) than products (on the right). This is consistent only with answer (C). Answer (A) shows a double-replacement reaction (in which two sets of ions switch bonds), answer (B) shows a synthesis reaction (in which there are fewer products than reactants), and answer (D) shows a single-replacement reaction (in which one substance replaces another in its bond, but the other does not get a new bond).

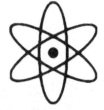

311. *General Science*

A long silver bar is 50°C at one end and 0°C at the other end. The bar will reach thermal equilibrium (the same temperature along the entire length of the bar), barring outside influence, by the process of heat _____.

A. conduction
B. convection
C. radiation
D. phase change

312. *General Science*

When you step out of the shower, the floor feels colder on your feet than the bathmat. Which of the following is the correct explanation for this?

A. The floor is colder than the bathmat
B. Your feet have a chemical reaction with the floor, but not with the bathmat
C. Heat is conducted more easily into the floor
D. Water is absorbed from your feet into the bathmat

313. *General Science*

When heat is added to most solids, they expand. Why?

A. The molecules get bigger
B. The faster molecular motion leads to greater distance between the molecules
C. The molecules develop greater repelling electric forces
D. The molecules form a more rigid structure

311. *General Science*

Answer: A. conduction

Heat conduction is the process of heat transfer via solid contact. The molecules in a warmer region vibrate more rapidly, jostling neighboring molecules and accelerating them. This is the dominant heat transfer process in a solid with no outside influences. Convection is heat transfer by way of fluid currents; radiation is heat transfer via electromagnetic waves; phase change can account for heat transfer in the form of shifts in matter phase.

312. *General Science*

Answer: C. Heat is conducted more easily into the floor

When you step out of the shower, your feet are warmer than either the floor or the bathmat. This heat can be transferred to either surface but since the hard surface (the floor) conducts heat more easily than the soft surface (the bathmat), the hard surface will feel colder as heat is transferred from your feet more quickly. The floor and the bathmat conduct heat at different rates because of differences in specific heat (the energy required to change temperature, which varies by material).

313. *General Science*

Answer: B. The faster molecular motion leads to greater distance between the molecules

The atomic theory of matter states that matter is made up of tiny, rapidly moving particles. These particles move more quickly when warmer, because temperature is a measure of average kinetic energy of the particles. Warmer molecules therefore move further away from each other, with enough energy to separate from each other more often and for greater distances.

314. *General Science*

The number of atoms in $2H_2SO_4$ is:

A. 7
B. 14
C. 2
D. 3

315. *General Science*

Which parts of an atom are located inside the nucleus?

A. Protons and electrons
B. Protons and neutrons
C. Protons only
D. Neutrons only

316. *General Science*

Blue litmus paper turns pink when exposed to which of the following?

A. An acid
B. A base
C. An indicator substance
D. Light

314.
General Science

Answer: B. 14

H_2SO_4 is the chemical equation for sulfuric acid. The equation in the question represents 2 units of sulfuric acid. There are 4 hydrogen (2 x 2), 2 sulfur (2 x 1), and 8 oxygen atoms (2 x 4) in $2H_2SO_4$.

315.
General Science

Answer: B. Protons and neutrons

Protons (positively charged) and neutrons (neutral, no charge) are located in the nucleus, while electrons (negatively charged) move around outside the nucleus.

316.
General Science

Answer: A. An acid

An indicator is any substance used to assist in the classification of another substance. An example of an indicator is litmus paper that measures whether a substance is acidic or basic. Blue litmus turns pink when placed in an acid, and pink litmus turns blue when dipped in a base.

317.

General Science

The elements in the modern Periodic Table are arranged _____.

A. in numerical order by atomic number
B. randomly
C. in alphabetical order by chemical symbol
D. in numerical order by atomic mass

318.

General Science

The chemical equation for water formation is: $2H_2 + O_2 \rightarrow 2H_2O$. Which of the following is an INCORRECT interpretation of this equation?

A. Two moles of hydrogen gas and one mole of oxygen gas combine to make two moles of water
B. Two grams of hydrogen gas and one gram of oxygen gas combine to make two grams of water
C. Two molecules of hydrogen gas and one molecule of oxygen gas combine to make two molecules of water
D. Four atoms of hydrogen (combined as a diatomic gas) and two atoms of oxygen (combined as a diatomic gas) combine to make two molecules of water

---

319.

General Science

The half-life of a radioactive isotope is 8 days. How long will it take for 10 milligrams of this isotope to decay to 1.25 milligrams?

A. 8 days
B. 12 days
C. 32 days
D. 24 days

317.

Answer: A. in numerical order by atomic number

Although the first periodic tables were arranged by atomic mass, the modern table is arranged by atomic number, i.e., the number of protons in each element. It is the atomic number which determines what the element is.

318.

Answer: B. Two grams of hydrogen gas and one gram of oxygen gas combine to make two grams of water

In any chemical equation, the coefficients (the numbers before the letters) indicate the relative proportions of atoms, molecules or moles of molecules. They do not refer to mass. Answer (B) incorrectly refers to grams, a unit of mass.

319.

Answer: D. 24 days

If the half-life is 8 days, this means that every 8 days the amount is reduced in half. Starting with 10 milligrams gives us: 5 milligrams in 8 days; 2.5 milligrams in 16 days; 1.25 milligrams in 24 days.

320.   *General Science*

Which of the following statements describes an isotope of an element?

A. An isotope has a different number of electrons
B. An isotope has a different number of neutrons
C. The arrangement of the electrons is different
D. An isotope has a different number of protons

---

321.   *General Science*

Physical properties are observable characteristics of a substance in its natural state. Which of the following are considered physical properties?

I Color, II Density, III Specific gravity, IV Melting Point

A. I only
B. I and II only
C. I, II, and III only
D. III and IV only

---

322.   *General Science*

Which of the following is an example of a chemical change?

A. Freezing food to preserve it
B. Using baking powder in biscuits
C. Melting glass to make a vase
D. Mixing concrete with water

320.

General Science

Answer: B. An isotope has a different number of neutrons

A change in the number of electrons (A) creates an ion. The change in the arrangement of the electrons (C) could change the reactivity of an atom temporarily. A change of the number of protons, answer (D), will change the atom into a new element. Answer (B) is the only one that does not change the relative charge of an atom, while changing the weight of an atom, which in essence is what an isotope is.

321.

General Science

Answer: C. I, II, and III only

Color is readily observable. Density can be measured without changing a substance's form or structure. Specific gravity is a ratio of the density of a substance to the density of water and can be calculated. Of the choices given, only the melting point of a substance cannot be found without altering the substance itself, i.e., it is not a directly observable characteristic.

322.

General Science

Answer: B. Using baking powder in biscuits

A physical change is a change that does not produce a new substance. The freezing and melting of water is an example of physical change. A chemical change (or chemical reaction) changes the inherent properties of a substance. Examples include burning materials turning into smoke and ash; seltzer tablets fizzling into gas bubbles when submerged in water; and baking powder releasing carbon dioxide into dough to raise it.

323.   *General Science*

When is a hypothesis formed?

A. Before the data is collected
B. After the data is collected
C. After the data is analyzed
D. While the data is being graphed

324.   *General Science*

In an experiment measuring the growth of bacteria at different temperatures, what is the independent variable?

A. Number of bacteria
B. Growth rate of bacteria
C. Temperature
D. Light intensity

325.   *General Science*

A student grew two plants in 50% light and two plants in 100% light and measured photosynthetic rates by measuring the plant mass. Which of the following is the control in the experiment?

A. Plants grown with no added nutrients
B. Plants grown in the dark
C. Plants grown in 100% light
D. Plants grown in 50% light

323. *General Science*

Answer: A. Before the data is collected

A hypothesis is an educated guess, made before undertaking an experiment. The purpose of performing an experiment is to test the hypothesis. After the experimental data is collected, the hypothesis is reevaluated against the collected data. Therefore, the hypothesis must be formed before the data is collected, not during or after the experiment.

324. *General Science*

Answer: C. Temperature

The independent variable in an experiment is the item that is changed by the scientist, in order to observe the effects of the change on the dependent variable/s. In this experiment, temperature is changed in order to measure growth of bacteria, so temperature is the independent variable and the growth of bacteria is the dependent variable.

325. *General Science*

Answer: C. Plants grown in 100% light

A control is a factor that remains unchanged throughout an experiment and allows the researcher to verify that the experiment worked correctly. When using a control, all the conditions are the same except for the variable being tested. A control is needed in every experiment; it is necessary to prove that the results obtained are a result of the manipulated variable. Only one variable should be manipulated at a time. The plants grown in 100% light are the control that the student will compare with the growth of the plants in 50% light.

326. *Mechanical Comprehension*

When a car is hit from behind, a passenger's head is thrown backward causing a whiplash injury. This happens because:

A. Inertia causes the head to stay in the same place while the body, in contact with the car, accelerates forward
B. The head is moved backward by the force from behind while the body, due to inertia, stays in the same place
C. Inertia causes the head to move backward while the body, in contact with the car, accelerates forward
D. Inertia causes the head to move forward while the body, in contact with the car, accelerates backward

327. *Mechanical Comprehension*

How much force is needed to accelerate a ball of mass 100g at 2.5 m/s^2?

A. 40 N
B. 250 N
C. 0.25 N
D. 4 N

328. *Mechanical Comprehension*

When you jump, you exert a force on the earth and the earth exerts a force on you that lifts you up. Which force is greater, the one with which you push down on the earth or the one with which the earth pushes you up?

A. The forces are equal
B. The force on the earth is greater
C. The force on you is greater
D. Which force is greater depends on how you are jumping

326.   *Mechanical Comprehension*

Answer: A. Inertia causes the head to stay in the same place while the body, in contact with the car, accelerates forward

As stated in Newton's first law of motion, inertia is the tendency of an object to stay in a state of rest or in uniform motion unless acted upon by another force. When a car is hit from behind, the body is in contact with the car and so it moves forward in response to the external force. If there is no headrest, the head is not in contact with the car and so it stays in place while the body moves forward, effectively sending it backwards and causing whiplash.

327.   *Mechanical Comprehension*

Answer: C. 0.25 N

According to Newton's second law of motion, Force = mass x acceleration (F = ma)

The unit of force is the Newton (N) and it is expressed in terms of kilograms times meters per second squared (N = Kg m/s^2) so the first step in calculating force is to convert the 100g mass of the ball to kilograms: 100g = 0.1 Kg.

Force = 0.1 Kg x 2.5 m/s^2 = 0.25 N

328.   *Mechanical Comprehension*

Answer: A. The forces are equal

According to Newton's third law of motion, every action has an equal and opposite reaction. When you push down on the earth, the earth exerts an equal upward force on you.

329.   *Mechanical Comprehension*

A car speeds up uniformly from 0 to 60 Km/hr in 10 seconds. What is its acceleration?

A. 6 m/s^2
B. 6000 m/s^2
C. 0.002 m/s^2
D. 1.67 m/s^2

---

330.   *Mechanical Comprehension*

When an object moves in a circle with uniform speed its acceleration is:

A. Zero
B. Directed towards the center of the circle
C. Directed away from the center of the circle
D. Tangential to the circle

---

331.   *Mechanical Comprehension*

A flywheel rotates 30,000 times a minute. Its frequency is:

A. 3000 Hz
B. 500 Hz
C. 1500 Hz
D. 600 Hz

329.   *Mechanical Comprehension*

Answer: D. 1.67 m/s^2

The acceleration of the car = $\dfrac{V - V_0}{t}$ where v is the final velocity, V_0 is the initial velocity and t is the time interval.

Acceleration is expressed in meters per second squared (m/s^2), so the first step is to express the kilometers per hour as meters per second. 1 Km/1hr = 1000 m/3600 s, so 60 Km/hr = 60,000 m/3600 s

Acceleration = (60,000 m/3600 s) ÷ 10 s
= (60,000 m/3600 s) x (1/10 s)
= 60,000 m/36,000 s^2
= 1.67 m/s^2

---

330.   *Mechanical Comprehension*

Answer: B. Directed towards the center of the circle

The acceleration of an object in uniform circular motion is directed towards the center of the circle and is known as centripetal acceleration.

---

331.   *Mechanical Comprehension*

Answer: B. 500 Hz

The frequency of the flywheel in Hz =
$\dfrac{30,000 \text{ cycles}}{60 \text{ seconds}} = 500 \text{Hz}$

332. *Mechanical Comprehension*

A heavy crate with a mass of 200 Kg is sitting on a concrete warehouse floor. If it takes a force of 1176N to get it to start sliding, then:

A. The coefficient of static friction between the floor and crate is 0.5
B. The coefficient of kinetic friction between the floor and crate is 0.5
C. The coefficient of static friction between the floor and crate is 0.6
D. The coefficient of kinetic friction between the floor and crate is 0.6

---

333. *Mechanical Comprehension*

A man is standing completely still with a heavy box of books in his arms. The amount of work done by the man on the box is:

A. Equal to the weight of the box
B. The weight of the box times the height of the box
C. The weight difference between the man and the box times the height of the box
D. None

---

334. *Mechanical Comprehension*

A 50 Kg woman runs up a flight of stairs in 6 seconds. If the height of the stairs is 5 m, what is the woman's power output?

A. 2450 Joules
B. 2450 Watts
C. 403.8 Watts
D. 0 Watts

332.

Answer: C. The coefficient of static friction between the floor and crate is 0.6

The force of static friction must be overcome to get the box to move. The formula for static friction is: $F = \mu_s F_N$ where μ_s is the coefficient of static friction between the floor and the crate and F_N is the normal force exerted by the crate on the floor.

First calculate the normal force (F = ma) using the mass of the crate and the acceleration due to gravity, a constant (9.8 m/s^2):
F_N = 200Kg x 9.8 m/s^2 = 1960 N

Now find μ_s by rearranging the formula for static friction: μ_s = F/F$_N$

μ_s = 1176/1960 = 0.6.

333.

Answer: D. None

Work is done on an object when an applied force moves across a distance. Since the box held in the man's arms does not move, its displacement is zero and the work done on it is also zero.

334.

Answer: C. 403.8 Watts

Work is the transfer of energy by a force to move an object a certain distance. The standard unit for work or energy is the Joule. 1 Joule is defined as the work done when a force of 1 Newton is applied through a distance of 1 meter.

The woman has to overcome the force of gravity in order to move her body up the stairs. The force of gravity on the woman is equal to her weight x the acceleration due to gravity = 50 Kg x 9.8 m/s^2 = 490 N.

The amount of work done by the woman against gravity = force of gravity x vertical distance = 490 N x 5 m = 2450 Joules. Power is the work done, divided by the amount of time it took to do it. Since the work is done in 6 seconds, power output = 2450 Joules/ 6 s = 408.3 Watts.

335. *Mechanical Comprehension*

A ball is tossed straight upwards. When it is at its highest point, assuming air resistance is negligible, its mechanical energy is:

A. All potential
B. All kinetic
C. Partly potential and partly kinetic
D. A mix of potential, kinetic, and other kinds of energy

336. *Mechanical Comprehension*

A spring has a spring constant of 75 N/m. How much force is needed to keep the spring stretched out 5 cm from its normal position?

A. 375 N
B. 3.75 N
C. 18.75 N
D. 9.38 N

337. *Mechanical Comprehension*

A 1200 Kg car moving at a speed of 30 Km/hr collides with another car that is at rest. If both cars stick together and keep moving in the same direction at 10 Km/hr, what is the mass of the second car?

A. 2400 Kg
B. 3600 Kg
C. 1200 Kg
D. 1800 Kg

335.
Mechanical Comprehension

Answer: A. All potential

When the ball is tossed directly upwards, its initial mechanical energy is all kinetic energy. As it moves upwards it slows down, reducing its kinetic energy and converting the remaining energy to potential energy. At the highest point, the ball is at rest with zero kinetic energy and all its mechanical energy in the form of potential energy. As the ball falls back down to earth, the proportion of kinetic energy increases as it accelerates until the energy is all kinetic just before it hits the ground.

While the ball is in the air, its mechanical energy is conserved, i.e., the sum of its energy is constant, even though the relative amounts of kinetic and potential energy is shifting.

336.
Mechanical Comprehension

Answer: B. 3.75 N

In order to keep the spring stretched out from its normal position, the restoring force of the spring must be overcome. The restoring force is the force that moves the spring back to its normal position and is given by the formula $F = -kx$ where k is the spring constant and x is the displacement of the spring from its normal position.

First, calculate the restoring force, $F = -(75 \text{ N/m})(0.05 \text{ m}) = -3.75\text{N}$. The minimum force needed to oppose this is 3.75 N.

337.
Mechanical Comprehension

Answer: A. 2400 Kg

Momentum (p) equals mass x velocity and is given by the formula $p = mv$.

The total momentum of the two-car system before the collision = (1200 Kg)(30 Km/hr) + (x Kg)(0 Km/hr) = 36,000 Kg Km/hr.

According to the principle of conservation of momentum, the total momentum of the system remains the same after the collision as it was before the collision. We can use this to find the mass of the second car.

36,000 Kg Km/hr = (1200 Kg)(10 Km/hr) + (x Kg)(10 Km/hr)
36,000 Kg Km/hr = (12,000 Kg Km/hr) + (10x Kg Km/hr)
24,000 Kg Km/hr = 10x Kg Km/hr
x = 2400 Kg

338.
Mechanical Comprehension

The graph below shows the displacement of an object over a 15 second time span. From this graph we can tell that the velocity of the object over the time span, in sequence, was:

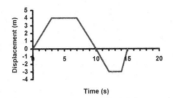

A. Positive and then negative
B. Positive, zero, negative
C. Negative, zero, positive, zero, negative
D. Positive, zero, negative, zero, positive

339.
Mechanical Comprehension

The graph below shows the displacement of an object over a 15 second time span. At time 12s, the:

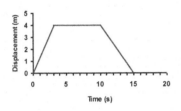

A. Velocity was negative and acceleration was zero
B. Velocity was positive and acceleration was zero
C. Velocity was negative and acceleration was positive
D. Velocity was negative and acceleration was negative

340.
Mechanical Comprehension

A car travels to a town 100 miles due west at 50 mph and returns to its starting point along the same road at 60 mph. The average velocity of the car for the entire trip is:

A. 55 mph
B. 54.5 mph
C. 58 mph
D. 0 mph

338.

Mechanical Comprehension

Answer: D. Positive, zero, negative, zero, positive

The velocity of an object is the rate of change of its displacement. Therefore, on a graph showing displacement vs. time, the velocity at any point in time is the slope of the line at that point.

From the graph we see that the slope of the line is initially positive (since displacement increases with time), then zero (no change in displacement for a few seconds, giving a flat line), then negative (displacement decreases with time), then zero again and then positive again.

339.

Mechanical Comprehension

Answer: A. Velocity was negative and acceleration was zero

On a graph showing displacement vs. time, the velocity at any point in time is the slope of the line at that point. At time 12s, that section of the graph is a line with a negative slope (displacement decreases with time) so the velocity is negative.

Acceleration is the rate of change of velocity. Since the graph of the displacement is a straight line with constant slope from 10s to 15s, the velocity does not change during that time period and the acceleration is zero.

340.

Mechanical Comprehension

Answer: D. 0 mph

The average velocity is not the same as average speed. Average speed is the total distance traveled divided by the total time taken. Average velocity is the net displacement divided by the total time taken. Since the car returns to its starting point at the end of the trip, its net displacement is zero. Therefore its average velocity is also zero.

341. *Mechanical Comprehension*

The mechanical advantage of a machine is the ratio of:

A. Output force to input force
B. Output force to input energy
C. Output energy to input force
D. Output energy to input energy

---

342. *Mechanical Comprehension*

Which of the following is a compound machine?

A. An inclined plane
B. A wheel and axle
C. A pair of pliers
D. A pulley

---

343. *Mechanical Comprehension*

A mover moves furniture along a 4.5m ramp up to a moving van that is 1.5m high. What is the ideal mechanical advantage of the ramp?

A. 4
B. 3
C. 4.5
D. 6

341.

Mechanical Comprehension

Answer: A. Output force to input force

The mechanical advantage of a machine is defined as the ratio of the output force to the input force. The smaller the input force needed to move a load, the higher the mechanical advantage of the machine. Due to the law of conservation of energy, you cannot get more energy out of a machine than you put into it.

342.

Mechanical Comprehension

Answer: C. A pair of pliers

A compound machine is one made up of two or more simple machines. The six types of simple machines are lever, pulley, inclined plane, wheel and axle, wedge and screw. A pair of pliers is made of two levers and is therefore a compound machine.

343.

Mechanical Comprehension

Answer: B. 3

Ideal mechanical advantage is the mechanical advantage of a system assuming there is no energy loss to friction or any other dissipative force.

For an inclined plane, the ideal mechanical advantage (IMA) = length of plane/height of the topmost point (i.e., length of the ramp/vertical distance)

In this case, IMA = 4.5m/1.5m = 3.

344.   *Mechanical Comprehension*

A mover has to apply a force of 300N to move a couch of mass 95 Kg up a ramp that has an ideal mechanical advantage (IMA) of 4. What is the efficiency of the ramp?

A. 310%
B. 129%
C. 78%
D. 100%

---

345.   *Mechanical Comprehension*

The following is an example of a second class lever:

A. Human arm
B. Wheelbarrow
C. Seesaw
D. Crowbar

---

346.   *Mechanical Comprehension*

A first class lever is 1m long. The fulcrum is 0.4m from the load end. What is its mechanical advantage?

A. 0.67
B. 6
C. 1.5
D. 2.5

344.   *Mechanical Comprehension*

Answer: C. 78%

The actual mechanical advantage (AMA) of the system = output force/input force.

The output force is the mass of the couch x the acceleration due to gravity = 95 Kg x 9.8m/s^2 = 931N.

AMA = 931N/300N = 3.103.

The efficiency of the ramp = AMA/IMA x 100% = (3.103/4) x 100% = 78%.

---

345.   *Mechanical Comprehension*

Answer: B. Wheelbarrow

In a first class lever, the fulcrum is between the input (effort) and output (load). In a second class lever, the load is between the fulcrum and effort. In a third class lever, the effort is between the fulcrum and load.

A wheelbarrow is an example of a second class lever since the fulcrum is at one end, the handle where the effort is put in is at the other end, and the load is in the middle. A human arm is a third class lever while a seesaw and crowbar are both first class levers.

---

346.   *Mechanical Comprehension*

Answer: C. 1.5

The mechanical advantage of a lever is the ratio of its effort arm (distance from fulcrum to effort point) to its load arm (distance from fulcrum to load point):
Lever MA = effort arm/load arm

In this case the load arm = 0.4m and the effort arm = 1m – 0.4m = 0.6m.

The mechanical advantage = 0.6/0.4 = 1.5.

347.

Mechanical Comprehension

What force F should be applied at the other end of the lever to keep the beam balanced on the fulcrum?

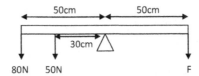

A. 110N
B. 130N
C. 65N
D. 78N

348.

Mechanical Comprehension

A 50N effort must be applied to a frictionless wheel and axle system to lift a load of 200N. The system can be modified to lift a load of 400N with a 50N effort by:

A. Doubling the radii of both the wheel and axle
B. Doubling the radius of the wheel
C. Doubling the radius of the axle
D. Halving the radius of the wheel

349.

Mechanical Comprehension

The pulley system shown in the diagram below is used to lift a crate of mass M. If g is the acceleration due to gravity, what force F must be applied to the end of the rope to move the crate up at constant speed? Assume the pulleys are frictionless and massless.

A. Mg
B. Mg/2
C. 2Mg
D. Mg/3

347.

Mechanical Comprehension

Answer: A. 110N

The net torque on one side of the beam must balance the net torque on the other side: F x d = F x d

The torque due to the 80N force = 80 x 50 N cm.
The torque due to the 50N force = 50 x 30 N cm.

To balance the torques we must have (80 x 50) + (50 x 30) = (F x 50)

Solving the equation for F:
50F = 4000 + 1500
50F = 5500
F = 110N

348.

Mechanical Comprehension

Answer: B. Doubling the radius of the wheel

Mechanical advantage can be expressed as a ratio of load to effort:
MA = load/effort

The mechanical advantage of this wheel and axle system = 200N/50N = 4.

Since the MA of a wheel and axle can also be expressed as a ratio of the radii of the wheel and axle, we know that: Radius of the wheel (R_W)/Radius of the axle (R_A) = 4.

If the system is modified to lift double the load (400N) with the same effort (50N), the mechanical advantage will be 400N/50N = 8. To achieve this, the radii must be modified so that R_W/ R_A = 8. Only choice B will result in this ratio.

349.

Mechanical Comprehension

Answer: B. Mg/2

F   F

Mg

Consider the forces on the lower pulley. There is a downward force on it of magnitude Mg due to the weight of the crate and the acceleration due to gravity g. The two upward forces on it are due to the tension in the rope and both are equal to the force F applied to the rope. If the pulley and crate move upwards at constant speed, the net force on them must be zero, i.e., the upward force must balance the downward force. Hence, 2F = Mg and F = Mg/2.

350. *Mechanical Comprehension*

What is the ideal mechanical advantage of the block and tackle system shown below?

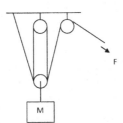

A. 1
B. 2
C. 3
D. 4

---

351. *Mechanical Comprehension*

The mechanical advantage of a fixed pulley is:

A. 1
B. 2
C. 3
D. 4

---

352. *Mechanical Comprehension*

A belt and pulley system has a small pulley with a 2 inch radius and a large pulley with a 6 inch radius. If the small pulley rotates at 2400 rpm, what is the rotational speed of the large pulley?

A. 7200 rpm
B. 1600 rpm
C. 4800 rpm
D. 800 rpm

350. *Mechanical Comprehension*

Answer: D. 4

The ideal mechanical advantage of a block and tackle or multiple pulley system is equal to the number of ropes attached to the movable part. Since 4 ropes are supporting the moveable pulley shown in the diagram, the mechanical advantage of this system is 4.

351. *Mechanical Comprehension*

Answer: A. 1

A fixed pulley does not reduce the effort needed to pull a load across it. The effort is equal to the load, hence the mechanical advantage is 1. The function of a fixed pulley is to reverse the direction of the force, in many cases allowing the user to take advantage of the force of gravity.

352. *Mechanical Comprehension*

Answer: D. 800 rpm

The circumference of a circle is given by the formula 2πr. Since the small pulley has a radius r of 2 inches, the distance any point on its surface moves in 1 minute =
$2400 \times 2\pi r = 2400 \times 2\pi(2) = 9600\pi$ inches.

Since both pulleys are connected by a belt, any point on the large pulley must also move the same distance in 1 minute.

Therefore, if the rotational speed of the large pulley is ω, then
$\omega \times 2\pi(6) = 9600\pi$; or $\omega = \dfrac{9600}{12} = 800$ rpm.

353. *Mechanical Comprehension*

One major difference between a belt and pulley system and gears is that:

A. In a belt and pulley system the input and output axles rotate in the same direction
B. In a belt and pulley system the input and output axles rotate in opposite directions
C. Unlike gears, belt and pulley systems are not used to change the speed of rotating axles
D. Unlike the gear ratio, the ratio of the pulley diameters is not significant in a belt and pulley system

---

354. *Mechanical Comprehension*

Three parallel gears are meshed together in a gear train. Which of the following is true?

A. The last gear in line rotates in the same direction as the first gear
B. The last gear in line rotates in the same direction as the second gear
C. The second gear in line rotates in the same direction as the first gear
D. The last gear in line rotates in the direction opposite to the first gear

---

355. *Mechanical Comprehension*

A gear with 20 teeth rotating at 500 rpm is driving a gear with 50 teeth. What is the rotational speed of the second gear?

A. 1250 rpm
B. 1600 rpm
C. 200 rpm
D. 800 rpm

353.

Answer: A. In a belt and pulley system the input and output axles rotate in the same direction

In a belt and pulley system, the driving or input pulley rotates in the same direction as the output pulley. For gears, on the other hand, the output axle rotates in a direction opposite that of the input axle.

354.

Answer: A. The last gear in line rotates in the same direction as the first gear

In a gear train, each gear rotates in a direction opposite to the gear driving it. Therefore, the second gear in line rotates in a direction opposite to the first gear. The third gear in line rotates in a direction opposite to the second gear which is the same direction as the first gear rotates.

355.

Answer: C. 200 rpm

When two gears are meshed, the product of the rotational speed and number of teeth of each gear is the same, i.e.,

$$\omega_1 t_1 = \omega_2 t_2 \quad ; \quad \omega_2 = \frac{\omega_1 t_1}{t_2}.$$

In this problem ω_1 = 500 rpm, t_1 = 20 and t_2 = 50.
Hence,

$$\omega_2 = \frac{500 \times 20}{50} = 200 \, \text{rpm}$$

356. *Mechanical Comprehension*

Marching soldiers break step when crossing a bridge in order to:

A. Avoid setting up a resonant vibration in the bridge
B. Avoid putting extra pressure on the bridge
C. Avoid increasing the natural frequency of the bridge
D. Avoid damping the vibrations on the bridge

357. *Mechanical Comprehension*

The length of time it takes for a simple pendulum (a weight hanging at the end of a string) to complete one swing will change if:

A. The weight hanging on the string is increased
B. The weight hanging on the string is decreased
C. The pendulum string is made longer
D. The pendulum is given a bigger initial push to start it moving

358. *Mechanical Comprehension*

The potential energy of a spring:

A. Increases when it is stretched and decreases when it is compressed
B. Decreases when it is stretched and increases when it is compressed
C. Increases when it is stretched and when it is compressed
D. Decreases when it is stretched and when it is compressed

356. *Mechanical Comprehension*

Answer: A. Avoid setting up a resonant vibration in the bridge

Any system, such as a swing or a bridge, vibrates at certain natural frequencies. If an external force is applied at a frequency that matches the natural frequency, the amplitude of vibration can become very large. This is known as resonance. Resonant vibration has caused bridges to collapse in the past. Resonance of the bridge with wind gusts was a factor in the collapse of the Tacoma Narrows Bridge in 1940.

357. *Mechanical Comprehension*

Answer: C. The pendulum string is made longer

The period of a simple pendulum, or the length of time it takes for it to complete one swing, depends only on the length of the string, not on the weight hanging at the end or on the initial force.
The period T of a simple pendulum is given by the formula

$T = 2\pi\sqrt{\dfrac{L}{g}}$ where L is the length of the pendulum and g =

9.8 m/s^2, the acceleration due to gravity.

358. *Mechanical Comprehension*

Answer: C. Increases when it is stretched and when it is compressed

In order to keep the spring stretched out or compressed from its normal position, the restoring force of the spring must be overcome. The work done to overcome the restoring force is stored in the stretched or compressed spring as potential energy.

359. *Mechanical Comprehension*

Which of the following is not true?
The buoyant force on an object floating in a fluid:

A. Acts in a downward direction
B. Is equal in magnitude to the force of gravity acting on the body
C. Is equal in magnitude to the weight of the fluid displaced by the body
D. Occurs because the pressure in a fluid increases with depth

---

360. *Mechanical Comprehension*

Why does part of a floating iceberg stay above the water?

A. Ice is denser than water
B. Ice is less dense than water
C. An iceberg has an irregular shape
D. An iceberg has a large surface area

---

361. *Mechanical Comprehension*

When air is blown at a high speed across the top of a perfume atomizer, the perfume is pushed up the tube because:

A. The high speed raises the air pressure across the top
B. The high speed lowers the air pressure across the top
C. The high speed keeps air pressure unchanged across the top
D. None of the above

359. *Mechanical Comprehension*

Answer: A. Acts in a downward direction

According to Archimedes' principle, the buoyant force of an object immersed in a fluid is equal to the weight of the fluid displaced by the object. The buoyancy force is due to the pressure difference between the top and bottom surfaces of the object. For a floating object, the buoyant force is large enough to balance the force of gravity that would normally make it sink. Therefore the buoyant force acts in a direction opposite to gravity, i.e., upwards.

360. *Mechanical Comprehension*

Answer: B. Ice is less dense than water

According to Archimedes' principle, the buoyant force of an object immersed in a fluid is equal to the weight of the fluid displaced by the object.

Since ice is less dense than water, it has less mass than the same volume of water. Therefore a smaller volume of water is needed to balance the weight of the iceberg and the entire iceberg is not submerged.

361. *Mechanical Comprehension*

Answer: B. The high speed lowers the air pressure across the top

According to Bernoulli's principle, where the velocity of a fluid (air or liquid) is high, the pressure is low and vice versa. The high air speed across the top of a perfume atomizer reduces the air pressure at that point. Since this is lower than the normal air pressure on the surface of the liquid, it is pushed up through the tube.

362. *Mechanical Comprehension*

Capillary action of water in a thin glass tube occurs due to:

A. Adhesion between water and glass only
B. Surface tension of water only
C. Adhesion between water and glass and surface tension of water
D. Neither adhesion between water and glass nor surface tension of water

363. *Mechanical Comprehension*

Why does heating a glass jar with a tight metal lid make it easy to open?

A. The metal lid expands but the glass jar stays the same size when heated
B. The metal lid stays the same size but the glass jar contracts when heated
C. Both the metal lid and glass jar expand when heated but the lid expands much more
D. Both the metal lid and glass jar contract when heated but the jar contracts much more

364. *Mechanical Comprehension*

If the pressure of a quantity of gas within a closed system is P, its temperature T and its volume V, then according to the ideal gas law:

A. PVT is constant
B. PV/T is constant
C. PT/V is constant
D. P/VT is constant

362. *Mechanical Comprehension*

Answer: C. Adhesion between water and glass and surface tension of water

Capillary action is the ability of liquids to flow against gravity in narrow spaces such as thin glass tubes or in porous materials such as paper. The force of adhesion or attraction between the water molecules and glass molecules in a thin tube makes the water rise and stick to the glass at the sides of the tube. The surface tension of water keeps the surface intact at the higher level.

363. *Mechanical Comprehension*

Answer: C. Both the metal lid and glass jar expand when heated but the lid expands much more

Both the metal lid and glass jar expand when heated but the lid expands much more since all metals have a higher coefficient of thermal expansion than glass.

364. *Mechanical Comprehension*

Answer: B. PV/T is constant

According to the ideal gas law, for a fixed quantity of gas in a closed system, the product of the pressure P and volume V is proportional to the temperature T. Hence PV = kT where k is a constant, i.e., PV/T is constant.

365.

Levers, pulleys, inclined planes, wheel and axle systems, wedges, and screws are the six types of:

A. Compound machines
B. Third class levers
C. Perfect machines
D. Simple machines

365.

Answer: D. Simple machines

Levers, pulleys, inclined planes, wheel and axle systems, wedges, and screws are the six types of simple machines. Compound machines are made of two or more simple machines.

366.

This schematic symbol shows:

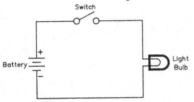

A. An AC voltage source
B. An open basic circuit
C. A closed parallel circuit
D. A closed basic circuit

367.

This schematic symbol shows:

A. A capacitor
B. A closed circuit
C. A diode
D. An inductor

368.

This schematic symbol shows:

A. A diode
B. An inductor
C. A resistor
D. A capacitor

366.

Answer: B. An open basic circuit

The circuit is basic because there is only one simple path for electrons to follow. However, the "load", or light bulb in this circumstance, will not function properly because the switch is in the open position. Electrons cannot flow through an open circuit.

367.

Answer: C. A diode

A diode symbol is an arrow that displays the direction of the electrical current. The function of the diode is to allow the current to go one way while blocking current from the opposite direction. The vertical line in front of the arrow displays the blocking of reverse electrical current.

368.

Answer: D. A capacitor

A capacitor symbol displays the space between two conductive plates that allow the build-up of electrons for various reasons. Capacitors are used to filter electrical energy, absorb voltage spikes in alternating current, and to quickly supply electrons where they are needed in complex circuits.

369. *Electronics Information*

This schematic symbol shows:

A. An inductor
B. A voltage meter
C. A basic circuit
D. A sine wave

370. *Electronics Information*

This schematic symbol shows:

A. An electrical current
B. A fuse within the circuit
C. A resistor within the circuit
D. An inductor within the circuit

371. *Electronics Information*

This schematic symbol shows:

A. A direct current voltage source
B. An alternating current voltage source
C. An oscillating current voltage source
D. A magnetic field voltage source

369.   *Electronics Information*

Answer: A. An inductor

This symbol shows an inductor as a coil of wire that produces a magnetic field. Often the wire is wrapped around a metal core, such as iron, increasing the magnetic field of the inductor. Schematic symbols of inductors may show a bar above the symbol for the wire coil signifying that there is a metallic core present.

370.   *Electronics Information*

Answer: C. A resistor within the circuit

The schematic symbol for a resistor displays an indirect path for electrons to follow that does not stop but slows down, or resists, the electrical current in a circuit.

371.   *Electronics Information*

Answer: A. A direct current voltage source

This symbol depicts a battery in a schematic diagram. A battery supplies a direct current to a circuit and has both positive and negative poles.

372. *Electronics Information*

This schematic symbol shows:

A. A magnetic field voltage source
B. A direct current voltage source
C. A diode within a complete circuit
D. An alternating current voltage source

---

373. *Electronics Information*

_____is the energy made available by the flow of electric charge through a conductor.

A. Inductance
B. Electricity
C. Resistance
D. Oscillation

---

374. *Electronics Information*

Conventional current occurs when:

A. Electrical current travels from the positive terminal around the circuit and back to the negative terminal.
B. Electrical current travels from the negative terminal around the circuit and back to the positive terminal.
C. Electrical current is pressured by capacitors along the circuit that oscillate the flow of electrons.
D. Electrical current is given a choice of two efficient paths to travel through a basic circuit.

372.

Answer: D. An alternating current voltage source

This symbol displays alternating current voltage sources using a sine wave. AC power sources each have a certain wavelength and frequency.

373.

Answer: B. Electricity

Electricity is associated with both stationary and moving electrons through a conductor.

374.

Answer: A. Electrical current travels from the positive terminal around the circuit and back to the negative terminal.

Much of the mathematics of modern electronics follows Benjamin Franklin's discovery that electricity usually flows from a positive to a negative. This is conventional current, whereas modern electronics utilizes electron paths depending upon the desired application.

375. *Electronics Information*

A useful electronic circuit must have three parts:

A. A capacitor, a diode, and an inductor
B. An oscillator, a DC voltage source, and a resistor
C. A voltage source, a conductor, and a load
D. A conductor, a resistor, and an insulator

---

376. *Electronics Information*

Any material that slows down a current in an electrical circuit is called:

A. A capacitor
B. A resistor
C. A diode
D. A connector

---

377. *Electronics Information*

A device that holds and stores energy in a circuit is called:

A. A capacitor
B. An insulator
C. A diode
D. An amplifier

375. *Electronics Information*

Answer: C. A voltage source, a conductor, and a load

A voltage source is needed to create the pressure that moves electrons through a conductor (this might be a metal like copper wire); the circuit is useful only when it does work, so there must be a load (like a light bulb or a machine) that receives the electrical current and performs a task.

376. *Electronics Information*

Answer: B. A resistor

All materials have a measurable resistance to electrical current. Some components are manufactured for their precise, measurable capabilities to cool, slow down, or resist electrical current in order to make a safer and more efficient circuit.

377. *Electronics Information*

Answer: A. A capacitor

Capacitors are important because they store energy and can be built to efficiently release energy. For these reasons capacitors are often found in power supplies. They also can amplify certain electrical frequencies in ways that can be controlled and measured.

378. *Electronics Information*

A capacitor's ability to store an electric charge is measured in:

A. Ohms
B. Volts
C. Amperes
D. Farads

379. *Electronics Information*

A semiconductor device used to amplify and switch electronic signals is a called:

A. A capacitor
B. A transistor
C. An oscillator
D. An inductor

380. *Electronics Information*

A device that increases the voltage, current, or power of a signal is called:

A. A conductor
B. An insulator
C. A resistor
D. An amplifier

378.

Answer: D. Farads

The farad is named after British scientist Michael Faraday who pioneered research into static electric fields and their capacity to hold energy in the early 19th century. Ohms are units of resistance. Volts measure electromotive force (EMF). Amperes measure the electrical current in a circuit.

379.

Answer: B. A transistor

A semiconductor is a material that allows electrons to flow through it, but at a very slow rate. Scientists add "impurities" to semiconductor materials, like silicon, to increase their conductivity. The transistor was created by building a tiny, three layered "sandwich", alternating negatively and positively charged semiconductor materials. The transistor can direct electricity, in very minute amounts, efficiently enough to perform a variety of functions at literally microscopic sizes. Human history was changed with the invention of the transistor in 1947.

380.

Answer: D. An amplifier

A conductor allows a path for electrons to follow. An insulator is a material that confines electrons to a predetermined path by protecting the circuit from coming into contact with other circuits. A resistor is anything that slows down the movement of electrons along a circuit path.

381. *Electronics Information*

A material that easily allows the flow of electrons through it while using only a small amount of voltage is called:

A. An inductor
B. A conductor
C. A capacitor
D. An oscillator

382. *Electronics Information*

Materials that do not conduct electricity well are also important in electronics. They may be used as:

A. Insulators
B. Capacitors
C. Oscillators
D. Diodes

383. *Electronics Information*

Inductors in an electronic circuit are devices that store energy in:

A. An electronic field
B. A capacitor
C. A magnetic field
D. An oscillating electronic field

381.

Electronics Information

Answer: B. A conductor

Conductors are the best materials to use when creating circuits to perform electrical functions. Metals are excellent conductors. The best are (in order of conductivity) silver, copper, gold, and aluminum.

382.

Electronics Information

Answer: A. Insulators

Insulators are used to shield electrical currents and to keep circuits safe. Frequently used industry-wide insulators include rubber, wax, porcelain, a variety of plastics, and glass.

383.

Electronics Information

Answer: C. A magnetic field

The most common inductors are made up of a wire coiled around a central core of iron. When electrons are pushed through this wire, it creates a magnetic field. Inductors are important because they store energy. Inductors can keep electrons moving long after the circuit has become open.

384. *Electronics Information*

The property that relates to the strength of the magnetic field produced by a coil of wire is called:

A. Resistance
B. Capacitance
C. Conductivity
D. Inductance

---

385. *Electronics Information*

A safety feature that opens, or "breaks", a circuit when too much voltage is applied is called:

A. A diode
B. A capacitor
C. A fuse
D. An ampere

---

386. *Electronics Information*

A device that allows current to flow in only one direction is called:

A. A diode
B. A resistor
C. A capacitor
D. An anode

384.   *Electronics Information*

Answer: D. Inductance

A coil with more inductance will produce a greater magnetic field than one with less inductance. Four factors determine the inductance of a coil: (1) the amount of coils, or turns, in the wire; (2) the closeness, or tightness, of the coil; (3) the coil diameter; and, (4) the material the coil is made of.

385.   *Electronics Information*

Answer: C. A fuse

A fuse usually contains a thin strip of metal held within an insulator that is connected to a circuit. When there is too much voltage applied to the circuit, the strip of metal heats up and melts, breaking the circuit. A fuse can stop a dangerous fire from occurring.

386.   *Electronics Information*

Answer: A. A diode

All diodes, which contain opposing anodes and cathodes, have a similar characteristic: they cause electrons to flow away from the anode to the cathode. The diode blocks any current from traveling from the cathode to the anode.

387.

Light emitting diodes, or LEDs, are important in electronics, and especially in circuits, because they display:

A. Magnetic fields occurring within the circuit
B. Oscillating current within a circuit
C. Electrical current moving through a circuit
D. When a fuse has melted and broken the circuit

388.

A device that provides a path for electrons to follow is called:

A. A magnetic field
B. A load
C. Voltage
D. A circuit

389.

When the path of electrons is interrupted in a circuit by a burned fuse or a switch that has been turned to the "off" position, we call this:

A. An open circuit
B. A closed circuit
C. A series circuit
D. A parallel circuit

ELECTRONICS INFORMATION

387.

Answer: C. Electrical current moving through a circuit

LEDs are illuminated solely by the movement of electrons so they are valuable in allowing us to see when an appliance is on, or whether a circuit is closed or open. LEDs do not contain a filament like an incandescent light, so they do not generate heat.

388.

Answer: D. A circuit

A circuit usually includes a voltage source, a conductor (often wire), and an object that performs an electrical function called a load (ex. a light bulb). All useful electrical circuits have these three basic elements.

389.

Answer: A. An open circuit

There must be a complete path for electrons to follow in order to create the opposite of an open circuit: the closed circuit. Only a closed circuit can accomplish the task of the circuit.

390. *Electronics Information*

A circuit that includes a voltage source, a conductor, and a load, and forms a complete path for electrons to follow is called:

A. An open circuit
B. A closed circuit
C. A series circuit
D. A parallel circuit

391. *Electronics Information*

A circuit in which all electrons must follow the same path, no matter how many loads there are on the circuit, is called:

A. A parallel circuit
B. An open circuit
C. A series circuit
D. Direct current

392. *Electronics Information*

An electrical circuit that has alternate paths for electrons to follow within a closed circuit is called:

A. A parallel circuit
B. An open circuit
C. A series circuit
D. Direct current

390.

Answer: B. A closed circuit

Electrons can flow only through a complete circuit. When the path has been interrupted, the opposite of a closed circuit is created, an open circuit.

391.

Answer: C. A series circuit

A series of lights that are illuminated along a single wire of electrical current is a good example of a series circuit. If one light burns out, however, the break in the path will cause an open circuit and none of the lights will work.

392.

Answer: A. A parallel circuit

Parallel circuits have two or more paths for electrons to travel within a closed, working circuit. The advantage of a parallel circuit is that, if there is a break along one of the paths, the circuit and the rest of its loads along the closed paths will keep working.

393.   *Electronics Information*

The electromotive force, or pressure, that causes electrons to move is called:

A. Current
B. Voltage
C. Inductance
D. Capacitance

---

394.   *Electronics Information*

The unit used to measure the electrical current within a circuit is called:

A. A watt
B. A coulomb
C. A volt
D. An ampere

---

395.   *Electronics Information*

Ohm's Law shows us the mathematical relationship of three elements within any electrical circuit. They are:

A. Voltage, resistance, and current
B. Voltage, capacitance, and inductance
C. Ohms, watts, and volts
D. Amperes, inductance, and current

393.

Answer: B. Voltage

Electrons need pressure, or a force, to move them. This is voltage. Current is the movement of electrons through a conductor, such as wire. Inductance has to do with magnetic fields. Capacitance is the potential to store electrons in a static state for further use.

394.

Answer: D. An ampere

A watt is a unit of power that describes how fast a circuit uses electrical energy. A coulomb measures an electric charge, or how fast a certain number of electrons flow through a single point in one second. A volt measures the electromotive force, or pressure, that moves electrons through a circuit.

395.

Answer: A. Voltage, resistance, and current

Georg Simon Ohm showed, in the early 19th century, that there is a mathematical relationship between the amount of voltage applied to a circuit, the resistance of the conductor within the circuit, and the amount of current flowing through the circuit. If two of these three variables are known, the third variable can be discovered using a mathematical equation.

396. *Electronics Information*

Ohm's Law can be displayed in the mathematical equation:

A. E rises = E1 + E2 + E3
B. E rises = E lowers
C. V = A + R
D. E = IR

397. *Electronics Information*

The unit used to measure resistance is:

A. The watt
B. The ohm
C. The ampere
D. The farad

398. *Electronics Information*

The unit of power that describes how fast a circuit uses electrical energy is:

A. A volt
B. A joule
C. A watt
D. A coulomb

396.

Answer: D. E = IR

The formula and variables in Ohm's Law are as follows: **E** (electromotive force, or voltage) equals **I** (for the French word intensité, meaning the electrical current) multiplied by **R** (resistance).

An easy way to remember this formula is the above drawing. Cover up the missing variable. Write the equation with the known numbers equaling the unknown. For example, if E and I are known but R is unknown, write: E/I=R.

397.

Answer: B. The ohm

The watt describes how fast a circuit uses electrical energy. The ampere is a unit describing the electrical current in a circuit. The farad measures capacitance.

398.

Answer: C. A watt

A volt is a unit used to measure electromotive force, or the pressure that moves electrons through a circuit. A joule is a unit of energy in the metric system. A coulomb measures an electric charge, or how fast electrons flow through a point in a circuit in one second.

399. *Electronics Information*

An instrument used to detect small electrical currents through a circuit is called:

A. A capacitor
B. A galvanometer
C. An inductor
D. A voltmeter

400. *Electronics Information*

A wire providing a conducting path independent of an appliance's normal electrical circuit path, useful in case of electrical fault, is called:

A. A hot wire
B. A neutral wire
C. A ground wire
D. A source of inductance

399.

Answer: B. A galvanometer

A galvanometer is a type of ammeter (an ammeter measures the number of amperes in a circuit) that is sensitive enough to measure very light electrical currents. A capacitor is a device that stores and delivers electrons within a complex circuit. An inductor is a device that provides a magnetic field. A voltmeter measures the amount of electromotive force within a circuit.

400.

Answer: C. A ground wire

A ground wire often leads from the case of an appliance and connects to the neutral wire in a plug in order to channel a potentially lethal electric shock away from the user. Appliances will work without a ground. However, a ground wire is used to re-channel a "fault" current, or an accidental contact between a "hot" wire and the appliance case.

401. *Shop Information*

Different types of hammers include:

A. Straight, curved, short and long handled
B. Metal working, woodworking, and cabinetry
C. Ball peen, claw, framing, finish, and brad
D. Fine, course, and detail

402. *Shop Information*

Choose the proper hammer for a task based on:

A. The type of nails to be used
B. The size of nails to be used
C. The type of materials to be used
D. All of the above

403. *Shop Information*

Nail gauge is determined by:

A. The type of head
B. The shape of head
C. The type of materials it's made of
D. The diameter of the nail

401.

Answer: C. Ball peen, claw, framing, finish, and brad

Each of these hammers is designed for a specific task. A ball peen hammer has a rounded head and is used for shaping sheet metal. Framing and finish hammers are both claw-type hammers. Framing hammers are used in rough framing and finish hammers are used for nailing on fine surfaces and cabinetry. A brad hammer is used when a small, lighter weight hammer is needed for fine nails and brads. Both finish and brad hammers are useful in reducing hammer marks on the surface of materials.

402.

Answer: D. All of the above

Different styles of hammers have varying weights, handle lengths and shapes, and head surface designs for different tasks. For example, a framing hammer with a checkered head would not be ideal for driving brads because brads are small nails for finish carpentry.

403.

Answer: D. The diameter of the nail

Nail gauge is measured in the same way as wire gauge, by the diameter of the nail. Gauge is determined by the number of an item (nails, sheets of metal, wires) it takes to make up an inch. For example, if 8 pieces of a given wire are placed side by side to make up an inch, that would be 8 gauge wire.

Nails may also be marked in pennies such as "10d" or "16d". The "d" is an old-English term that originally indicated the price in pennies for a hundred nails of that type. Today, the penny designates the standardized length of the nail. For example, a 16d common nail is 3.5" long with an 8 gauge shaft and head diameter of 11/32".

404. *Shop Information*

Types of nails include:

A. Brad
B. Finish
C. Common
D. All of the above

---

405. *Shop Information*

A jigsaw is used for:

A. Cutting jigs
B. Sawing metal
C. Cutting tight curves and small details
D. Only on wood

---

406. *Shop Information*

A rip saw is designed for:

A. Sawing fast
B. Sawing across the grain of wood
C. Sawing with the grain of wood
D. Sawing rough materials only

404.

Shop Information

Answer: D. All of the above

Brads, finish nails, and common nails are each intended for different purposes. Nail type is determined by gauge, length, head style, type of shank and the material it's made of. A brad is typically 20 gauge or smaller with a small finish-type head. Finish nails are larger than brads with a finish-type head and are used for fastening moldings and trim and where fasteners should be less visible in the finished work.

A finish-type nail head is only slightly larger than the gauge of the nail and has a dimple in the top of the head for use with a punch when recessing the nail into the wood. A common nail has a larger, flat head for better purchase on the materials being nailed and for ease of driving.

405.

Shop Information

Answer: C. Cutting tight curves and small details

Jigsaws use a narrow metal blade which allows them to cut tight curves and small details without binding in the wood. Selecting the proper blade allows the jigsaw to be used on any type of material.

406.

Shop Information

Answer: C. Sawing with the grain of wood

The teeth on a rip saw are coarser and give best results when sawing in the same direction as the grain.

407.   *Shop Information*

When cutting across the grain:

A. Use a pilot hole
B. Use a crosscut saw
C. Use both hands
D. Use a smaller saw

408.   *Shop Information*

Saw kerf is the:

A. Width of the material removed by the saw
B. Shape of the saw handle
C. Sound the saw makes when cutting
D. Number of teeth per inch

409.   *Shop Information*

Using a smooth-faced finish hammer reduces:

A. The effort required to nail
B. The strain on your wrist
C. Damage to the wood surface
D. The time it takes to nail

407.

Answer: B. Use a crosscut saw

The teeth on a crosscut saw are finer and create a cleaner finish when cutting across the wood fibers.

408.

Answer: A. Width of the material removed by the saw

Saw teeth protrude slightly to the left and right of the blade, cutting away a section slightly wider than the saw blade. This prevents the saw from binding in the cut and is called the kerf.

409.

Answer: C. Damage to the wood surface

The smooth face of a finish hammer leaves less damage on the surface of the wood around the nail.

410.   *Shop Information*

The checkered surface on the head of a rough framing hammer:

A. Limits slip when striking the nail head
B. Is designed for use with rough nails
C. Reduces the weight of the hammer
D. None of the above

---

411.   *Shop Information*

A lower grade number on sandpaper indicates:

A. A finer grit
B. A coarser grit
C. The type of grit material
D. A narrower sheet of sandpaper

---

412.   *Shop Information*

The grit on sandpaper is made from:

A. Garnet
B. Carborundum
C. Aluminum oxide
D. Any of the above

410.

Answer: A. Limits slip when striking the nail head

The traction provided by the checkered head of the framing hammer reduces the chance of slipping and bending nails.

411.

Answer: B. A coarser grit

The grade number of sandpaper indicates the size of the grit grains. Lower numbers indicate coarser grit and higher numbers indicate finer grit.

412.

Answer: D. Any of the above

The abrasive on sandpaper can be made from a variety of materials. Different grit types are intended for different surfaces. Harder materials like metal require a harder grit such as carborundum. Aluminum oxide can be used on metal but it wears out more quickly than carborundum. Both aluminum oxide and garnet hold up well when used on wood.

413. *Shop Information*

Screw types include:

A. Peen, offset, and square
B. Pan head, flat head, and sheet metal
C. Slot, Phillips, and Torx
D. Both B and C

414. *Shop Information*

Screw shank and ring shank nails are used because:

A. They won't split the wood
B. They can be driven with either a hammer or a screw driver
C. They have greater holding power than regular nails
D. They can be easily removed

415. *Shop Information*

Choose screws instead of nails to:

A. Draw materials together
B. Create a tighter bond between materials
C. In areas that may have a lot of motion or stress
D. All of the above

413.

Answer: D. Both B and C

Flat head screws are designed to seat flush with the surface. Pan head screws protrude from the materials they are fastening, but have a low profile.

Slot head screws use a single bladed screw driver. A Phillips head uses an x-tip screw driver. Torx screws use a 6-pointed star shaped driver.

Flat head screws are typically used in woodworking, pan head screws are typically used for fastening lath and sheet metal to framing and for metal work.

414.

Answer: C. They have greater holding power than regular nails

Both screw and ring shank nails grip the materials more securely and are less likely to work loose than standard nails.

415.

Answer: D. All of the above

Screws give a greater positive purchase on the materials they secure than nails do. Screws can be used to tighten loose areas and give more stability to areas that are subject to stress.

416. *Shop Information*

For a secure, permanent bond in wood, use:

A. Both nails and screws
B. Both staples and nails
C. Glue in addition to other fasteners
D. Wood shims and screws

417. *Shop Information*

In areas where fasteners should be invisible:

A. Use glue instead of nails or screws
B. Use a blind nailing or back nailing technique
C. Counter sink the fastener and plug with putty or wood doweling
D. Any of the above

418. *Shop Information*

In finish carpentry, avoid splitting hard woods when nailing or screwing by:

A. Wetting the wood before seating the fastener
B. Drilling a pilot hole
C. Using a dead blow hammer
D. Using an impact screw driver

416.

Answer: C. Glue in addition to other fasteners

Wood glue gives a secure permanent bond. For areas of high stress, use both wood glue and screws, nails, or other fasteners.

417.

Answer: D. Any of the above

There are many techniques that can be used when an aesthetic finish is required. Choose a technique based on the materials to be joined and the type of application.

418.

Answer: B. Drilling a pilot hole

Removing a small amount of material by drilling a pilot hole helps relieve stress on the wood. Hard grained woods can split when using nails or screws without a pilot hole.

419. *Shop Information*

Safety glasses should be worn:

A. Only when working with power tools
B. Whenever working with any type of tool
C. When in the same area as others who are working
with tools
D. Both B and C

420. *Shop Information*

A combination square is used for:

A. Measuring 90 and 45 degree angles
B. Measuring square objects
C. Scaling plans and blueprints
D. All of the above

421. *Shop Information*

Use a socket wrench when:

A. Gripping a screw head
B. A nut is hard to reach with pliers
C. Working on electrical sockets
D. Tightening a nut on a bolt

419.

Answer: D. Both B and C

Protect your eyesight whenever you are working with tools, or in an area where others are. Small bits of wood, metal, abrasives, and sawdust created by normal shop activities can travel surprisingly long distances.

420.

Answer: A. Measuring 90 and 45 degree angles

A combination square has built in surfaces for both 90 and 45 degree angles. The blade of the combination square is marked with a ruler and can be adjusted to show exact measurements. This can be used for drafting a line parallel to the edge of materials by sliding the square along an edge while marking the line. It's an excellent tool for checking the accuracy of square and 45 degree miter cuts.

421.

Answer: D. Tightening a nut on a bolt

Socket wrenches are used to seat bolts and nuts. They can also be used for driving lag bolts.

422.

SAE sockets include:

A. 3/16", 1/2", 5/8"
B. 8mm, 12mm, 13mm
C. 8 gauge, 10 gauge, 12 gauge
D. 8 penny, 10 penny, 16 penny

423.

A chuck key is used to:

A. Lock and unlock a tool kit
B. Replace the blade on a circular saw
C. Tighten or loosen the chuck on a drill or lathe
D. Measure a hole before drilling

424.

Pipe, crescent, strap, box and open end are types of:

A. Drivers
B. Pliers
C. Wrenches
D. Cutters

422.

Answer: A. 3/16", 1/2", 5/8"

SAE stands for the Society of Automotive Engineers, an organization that develops standards for tools used in the automotive and aerospace industries. SAE is sometimes referred to as English measurement units.

423.

Answer: C. Tighten or loosen the chuck on a drill or lathe

A chuck key is used to tighten or loosen the chuck jaws that hold a drill bit in the drill. On a lathe, the chuck is used to hold the material to be worked.

424.

Answer: C. Wrenches

The strap wrench is designed to grip finished surfaces without leaving marks. A pipe wrench is used for pipes and round shafts, but may damage the surface of the material being turned. A crescent wrench is a type of open end wrench with a "c" shape. Crescent wrenches may be adjustable, but open end wrenches are not. Many wrenches have an open end on one side and a box, or enclosed, end on the other. Use the box end of the wrench to prevent the wrench from slipping off the fastener.

425.   *Shop Information*

Channel locks, vice grips, lineman, and needle nosed are types of:

A. Drivers
B. Pliers
C. Dies and taps
D. Cutters

426.   *Shop Information*

When using a table saw, move the materials using:

A. A metal push rod
B. A wood push stick
C. Your left hand only
D. A saw fence

427.   *Shop Information*

Use a miter box to:

A. Brace square objects when gluing
B. Store your saw blades and chisels
C. Create a specific angle while sawing
D. Mark the position of pilot holes

425.

Answer: B. Pliers

Channel locks are adjustable to various sizes and are used like pipe wrenches but have less gripping ability. Vice grips are adjustable pressure pliers with a locking feature that is used for a more positive grip. They are also used to hold work in place while applying fasteners or welding. Lineman's pliers are used for pulling or bending wire and have a built-in wire cutter. Needle nose pliers are used in tight spaces where wider blade pliers won't fit.

426.

Answer: B. A wood push stick

For safety reasons, never push materials through a table saw using your hands. Always use a push stick to keep your fingers clear of the blade. Avoid using a push stick of hard materials like metal that might damage the saw blade if it comes into contact with it.

427.

Answer: C. Create a specific angle while sawing

Miter boxes are used to position a piece of material and guide the saw to create a specific angle cut. Miter boxes may have pre-set angles such as 90 and 45 degrees, or may be adjustable.

428. *Shop Information*

Levels are used for:

A. Making rough surfaces smooth
B. Checking for straightness
C. Checking an object to see if it is level
D. Finishing the surface of countertops and cabinets

429. *Shop Information*

A caliper is:

A. Used for drawing parallel lines on metal
B. Used for determining the measurement between two points
C. Part of a pneumatic drill
D. Used for scribing ovals and curves

430. *Shop Information*

Washers are used for:

A. Cleaning parts prior to assembly
B. Holding objects together
C. Covering large holes in parts for assembly
D. Enhancing the functionality of fasteners

428. *Shop Information*

Answer: C. Checking an object to see if it is level

The most commonly used level is the bubble level, where a bubble is visible inside a glass tube marked with calibrated lines. When the bubble is centered between the lines, the object being measured is level in the horizontal position.

Some levels are also designed to measure vertical plumb surfaces to ensure they are 90 degrees from horizontal. A string level, used for measuring relative level between two distant points, is a small bubble level designed to hang on a tensioned string or cord. Laser levels are replacing bubble levels for many applications because of their greater accuracy and ability to measure level over longer distances.

429. *Shop Information*

Answer: B. Used for determining the measurement between two points

A caliper is used to measure the distance between two points on an object. Specific calipers may be designed to measure the outside of objects, the inside of objects, the depth of an object, or a combination of all three. Mechanical calipers are used by fitting the measurement points across the object to be measured, removing the calipers from the object then measuring the distance between the points on a ruler. Many calipers have built-in rulers, dial gauges or digital readouts that show the measurement and can be read in metric or inch increments.

430. *Shop Information*

Answer: D. Enhancing the functionality of fasteners

Lock, star, flat and fender washers are different types of washers. Lock and star washers are typically used in metal work to prevent fasteners from working their way loose due to the stresses applied by moving parts. Flat washers can be used with wood, metal and plastics to increase the bearing area of the fastener; this prevents the fastener from imbedding itself too far into softer materials or pulling through entirely. Fender washers with a larger outside diameter are typically used with adjustable features such as slotted holes or when an exact alignment in parts is not needed.

431. *Automotive Information*

Smoke coming out the tail pipe might indicate:

A. The engine is burning oil
B. The engine is burning coolant
C. Normal condensation
D. Any of the above

432. *Automotive Information*

The proper sequence for tightening lug nuts on a wheel is:

A. Clockwise
B. Counterclockwise
C. Star or alternating pattern
D. The same way you took them off

433. *Automotive Information*

When an engine is burning coolant, the vapor coming out of the tail pipe smells:

A. Like gasoline
B. Sweet
C. Oily
D. Like burning charcoal

431.

Answer: D. Any of the above

Both oil and coolant will produce smoke when burned. Normal condensation can produce smoke-like vapors, especially when the engine or ambient temperature is cold.

432.

Answer: C. Star or alternating pattern

Tightening the lug nuts in a star or alternating pattern seats the wheel centrally on the studs and axel.

433.

Answer: B. Sweet

Coolants that contain ethylene glycol have a sweet smell that is especially pronounced when burned.

434. *Automotive Information*

The alternator:

A. Circulates air for better combustion
B. Alternates spark plugs for even wear
C. Charges the battery
D. Controls the windshield wiper speed

435. *Automotive Information*

Lug nuts should be:

A. Partially tightened and then re-tightened to torque specifications
B. Fully tightened before moving to the next nut
C. Tightened with your fingers
D. Tightened with pliers

436. *Automotive Information*

Rack and pinion is a type of:

A. Braking system
B. Suspension system
C. Steering system
D. Automotive lift system

434.

Answer: C. Charges the battery

The alternator senses the battery level and charges it when the battery level drops.

435.

Answer: A. Partially tightened and then re-tightened to torque specifications

The wheel will seat better against the brake hub when you partially seat all lug nuts, then retighten them in a star pattern. Using a torque wrench ensures that lug nuts are secured to the manufacturer's recommended settings.

436.

Answer: C. Steering system

Rack and pinion steering is used in high performance vehicles to give more responsive control with less motion of the steering wheel.

437. *Automotive Information*

Cupping on the tire means:

A. The tire sidewall has a bulge
B. The tread surface has an uneven dished-out wear pattern
C. The tread on one edge of the tire is worn out
D. The tire has tiny cracks in the rubber

438. *Automotive Information*

When using standard oil, most auto manufacturers suggest changing the engine oil:

A. Every other month
B. Every 3,000 to 7,500 miles, depending on the type of driving you do
C. When it looks black
D. When it gets too low

439. *Automotive Information*

Under inflated tires:

A. Reduce gas mileage
B. Wear out faster
C. Have better traction
D. Both A and B

437.

Answer: B. The tread surface has an uneven dished-out wear pattern

Cupping may be identified by an uneven or wave-like wear pattern on the surface of the tread.

438.

Answer: B. Every 3,000 to 7,500 miles, depending on the type of driving you do

Different types of driving create different types of wear on the engine. Changing the oil according to the manufacturer's guidelines helps to extend the life of the engine.

439.

Answer: D. Both A and B

Under inflated tires reduce gas mileage by increasing friction on the road. In addition, under inflation causes the tires to flex more, which causes them to heat up and wear more quickly.

440. *Automotive Information*

A serpentine belt is used to:

A. Turn the alternator
B. Operate the air conditioning compressor
C. Drive the power steering pump
D. All of the above

441. *Automotive Information*

The engine thermostat regulates:

A. Engine coolant temperature
B. Heater temperature
C. Air conditioning temperature
D. All of the above

442. *Automotive Information*

A timing light is used to:

A. Check the blink rate of turn signals
B. Check the engine timing
C. Determine engine RPM (revolutions per minute)
D. Check the speedometer accuracy

440. *Automotive Information*

Answer: D. All of the above

The serpentine belt is used to transfer energy from the crank shaft to other components in the engine. The serpentine belt may also drive the water pump, smog pump and radiator fan.

441. *Automotive Information*

Answer: A. Engine coolant temperature

The engine thermostat opens and closes to allow fluid to move between the radiator and the engine block to maintain safe engine operating temperatures.

442. *Automotive Information*

Answer: B. Check the engine timing

The timing light is used when adjusting the engine timing at the distributor. Correct timing is specified by the manufacturer as degrees below top dead center.

443. *Automotive Information*

The vacuum gauge is used to:

A. Check the air flow at the exhaust manifold
B. Adjust the Freon level in the air conditioning system
C. Check the pressure in the brake master cylinder
D. Check the vacuum pressure at the intake manifold or carburetor

444. *Automotive Information*

The compression tester is used to:

A. Check air conditioning output
B. Check cylinder pressure during the compression stroke
C. Check tire pressure
D. Check exhaust pressure at the tail pipe

445. *Automotive Information*

Optimum combustion requires:

A. Proper timing adjustment
B. Properly gapped and maintained spark plugs
C. Correct cylinder compression
D. All of the above

443.

Answer: D. Check the vacuum pressure at the intake manifold or carburetor

Vacuum pressure is used to operate many systems in the vehicle, including automatic transmission shifting, engine timing advance, breaking assist, air conditioning controls and emission control system.

444.

Answer: B. Check cylinder pressure during the compression stroke

The compression tester is used to check for the proper compression ratio on a piston, and to check for evenness between cylinders.

445.

Answer: D. All of the above

Optimum combustion occurs when the fuel delivery, electronic and mechanical systems in the engine are properly adjusted and in good repair.

446.

In a manual transmission, the clutch is used:

A. To engage the emergency brake while driving
B. To hold the wiring harness to the frame
C. To disengage power from the transmission while shifting gears
D. As a hand hold when accessing the roof rack on an SUV

447.

Using a higher transmission gear produces:

A. Lower travel speeds for the same engine RPM (revolutions per minute)
B. Higher travel speeds for the same engine RPM
C. A smoother ride around turns
D. Better handing on rough roads

448.

Radiator coolant should be checked:

A. When the engine is hot and running at idle speed
B. When the engine is off and cool
C. When the check engine light comes on
D. Every 12 months

446.

Answer: C. To disengage power from the transmission while shifting gears

In a manual transmission, the clutch disengages the power transfer from the engine to the transmission while the driver shifts between gears.

447.

Answer: B. Higher travel speeds for the same engine RPM

Each transmission gear is designed to produce a specific range of speed and torque while the engine is running in its optimum RPM range. Higher gears produce more rotations of the wheel for the same engine RPM.

448.

Answer: B. When the engine is off and cool

Opening the radiator while hot can release pressurized steam and result in burns. Wait until the engine has cooled before checking the radiator fluid levels.

449. *Automotive Information*

Squeaking or squealing engine belts may indicate:

A. Improper belt tension
B. The belt is worn and needs replacing
C. The belt is new and not broken in
D. Either A or B

---

450. *Automotive Information*

Drive train, suspension and wheel bearings:

A. May be sealed and not require maintenance
B. Require lubricant grease to operate correctly
C. May each require a different lubricant type
D. All of the above

---

451. *Automotive Information*

The connecting rod connects:

A. The lifter and the valve train
B. The piston and the crank shaft
C. The brake drum to the bearings
D. The engine to the frame

449.

Answer: D. Either A or B

Worn belts may stretch, loosen, harden or crack causing them to squeak. If the belt is in good condition, tightening the belt pulleys will usually stop the squeak.

450.

Answer: D. All of the above

All bearings require lubricant to operate correctly, however there are many different types of bearing configurations. Following the manufacturer's recommendations for lubrication type and maintenance schedule will prevent mechanical problems and excessive wear.

451.

Answer: B. The piston and the crank shaft

The connecting rod is connected to the piston head on one end and the crank shaft on the other. The connecting rod transfers energy from gas combustion to the drive train.

452.

The carburetor controls:

A. Engine timing and RPM
B. Fuel flow to the cylinders
C. Air flow to the cylinders
D. Both B and C

453.

The cam shaft:

A. Regulates the opening and closing of the intake and exhaust valves
B. Transfers power from the engine to the transmission
C. Connects the wheels to the drive train
D. Connects the steering wheel to the front axle

454.

The distributor is used to:

A. Adjust heater and air conditioning flow between vents
B. Make sure braking occurs on all four wheels
C. Deliver electrical power to the spark plugs for ignition in a specific sequence
D. Control power for each wheel in four wheel drive vehicles

452.

Answer: D. Both B and C

The carburetor mixes and adjusts the fuel and air flow into the cylinder. The fuel-air mix is controlled to provide maximum power at various speed and torque conditions.

453.

Answer: A. Regulates the opening and closing of the intake and exhaust valves

Lobes on the cam shaft operate the opening and closing of the intake and exhaust valves. The amount of lift and dwell (open) time for each valve is set by the specific size and shape of each lobe.

454.

Answer: C. Deliver electrical power to the spark plugs for ignition in a specific sequence

The distributor controls the timing of the spark that ignites the gas and air mixture in each cylinder. The spark should occur when the piston is just past the top of its stroke.

455. *Automotive Information*

Dieseling, where the engine continues to run after being turned off, may indicate:

A. Diesel fuel used instead of gas
B. Engine running too hot
C. Improper timing
D. Either B or C

456. *Automotive Information*

Tread that is worn down in the center of the tread pattern indicates:

A. Over inflated tires
B. Under inflated tires
C. Out of balance tires
D. All of the above

457. *Automotive Information*

Cupping on the tire may indicate:

A. Worn shock absorbers, struts or suspension components
B. Tire is over inflated
C. Tire is out of balance
D. Both A and C

455.

Answer: D. Either B or C

Dieseling occurs when fuel is ignited in the cylinder without a spark. Improper timing can cause incomplete fuel combustion, allowing the engine to continue to cycle. Overly high engine temperatures can ignite residual fuel in the cylinder.

456.

Answer: A. Over inflated tires

When a tire is over inflated, it rides on a narrow center section of the tread, reducing the contact area. Overinflated tires are unsafe because the smaller contact area decreases tire traction when breaking.

457.

Answer: D. Both A and C

Worn shock absorbers and struts allow the tire to bounce during normal driving. Out of balance tires may also bounce or vibrate causing a cupping wear pattern on the tire.

458.

Oily smelling smoke from the tail pipe may indicate:

A. Leaky valve stems
B. Leaky rings
C. Burned or cracked pistons
D. Any of the above

459.

Knocking in the engine is an indication of:

A. Poor timing adjustment
B. Failing bearings on the connecting rod or crank shaft
C. Improper octane level fuel for the engine
D. Any of the above

460.

In a four stroke engine the stroke sequence is:

A. Combustion, compression, intake, exhaust
B. Compression, combustion, intake, exhaust
C. Intake, combustion, compression, exhaust
D. Intake, compression, combustion, exhaust

458.

Answer: D. Any of the above

Oil can leak past damaged valve guides, rings or pistons into the combustion chamber of the cylinder. Smoky exhaust can result from oil burning along with the gasoline.

459.

Answer: D. Any of the above

Knocking can result from early detonation of the fuel in the cylinder due to poor timing or incorrect octane levels. Knocking may also indicate worn bearings on the connecting rod or crank shaft.

460.

Answer: D. Intake, compression, combustion, exhaust

In a four stroke engine, the first stroke draws in the fuel/air mixture, the second stroke compresses the fuel/air mixture, the third stroke is combustion where the piston transfers energy to the crank shaft, and the fourth stroke exhausts the combusted gasses.

461. *Automotive Information*

The internal combustion engine converts:

A. Motion to energy
B. The energy stored in oxygen to exhaust
C. The energy stored in petroleum to motion
D. Electrical energy to motion

462. *Automotive Information*

The power generated by the internal combustion engine comes from:

A. The turning of the crank shaft
B. Energy from the electronic spark
C. Pressure generated by the compression stroke
D. High temperature expanding gasses

463. *Automotive Information*

The Otto cycle:

A. Requires a spark plug to ignite the compressed air/fuel mixture
B. Is named after the inventor of the first four stroke piston-driven internal combustion engine
C. Is the thermodynamic cycle of the four stroke engine
D. All of the above

461.

Answer: C. The energy stored in petroleum to motion

The internal combustion engine converts the stored energy contained in petroleum into kinetic (movement) energy.

462.

Answer: D. High temperature expanding gasses

Hot gasses generated by the burning fuel push the piston down to turn the crank shaft.

463.

Answer: D. All of the above

Named for Nikolaus Otto, the Otto cycle describes the thermodynamic characteristics of the four stroke internal combustion engine. Otto cycle based engines use a spark plug to ignite the fuel/air mixture and have one power stroke (combustion stroke) in each four stroke cycle.

464. *Automotive Information*

An ideal air-fuel ratio:

A. Ensures all fuel in the cylinder is burned during combustion
B. Reduces air pollution
C. Improves MPG and engine efficiency
D. All of the above

---

465. *Automotive Information*

The air-fuel ratio for an internal combustion engine:

A. Depends on the engine load, altitude, and additives present in the fuel
B. Is less than 10:1
C. Is considered ideal at 14.7:1
D. Both A and C

---

466. *Automotive Information*

The gear ratio is the relationship between:

A. The number of 2-wheel drive and 4-wheel drive gears a car has
B. The gear shifter position and the speed of the car
C. The miles per gallon achieved while in a particular gear
D. The number of teeth on each of two meshed gears, resulting in the relative number of rotations for each gear

464.

Answer: D. All of the above

When the right amount of air is present to fully burn all fuel in the cylinder, the maximum amount of power is generated per cycle. Complete combustion of the fuel reduces gasses and unburned hydrocarbons that contribute to air pollution.

465.

Answer: D. Both A and C

The ideal air-fuel ratio is considered to be 14.7:1 (the air mass is equal to 14.7 times the fuel mass). Because this ratio can cause very high engine temperatures, a richer mixture (lower air-fuel ratio), is often used for acceleration and high load conditions. Factors such as altitude, which affects the available oxygen and air density, and fuel additives such as oxygenators (MTBE) can also alter the effective air-fuel ratio.

466.

Answer: D. The number of teeth on each of two meshed gears, resulting in the relative number of rotations for each gear

If the drive (input) gear has 10 teeth, and the driven (output) gear has 40 teeth, the ratio would be 4:1. For example, in the differential, the drive pinion would make 4 revolutions for each turn of the ring gear.

467.

A wheel rim of 13x6 is:

A. 13 inches in diameter and 6 inches wide at the bead seat
B. 13 inches in diameter and 6 inches wide at the outer flange
C. 13 inches in diameter and has a 6 lug pattern
D. Designed for a 13x6 tire

468.

The numbers 205/55/16 on the side of a tire are:

A. Tire model number / Tire speed rating (MPH) / Tire diameter (inches)
B. Tire width (mm) / Sidewall height (percentage of width) / Wheel rim diameter (inches)
C. Tire's treadwear rating /Maximum inflation pressure (PSI) / Tire radius (inches)
D. Rated tire life (times 100, in miles) / Tire width (mm) / Minimum tire pressure (PSI)

469.

The function of the cylinder is:

A. To contain the combustion reaction
B. To provide space for the movement of the piston
C. To decrease the weight of the engine block
D. Both A and B

467.

Answer: A. 13 inches in diameter and 6 inches wide at the bead seat

Rims are measured at the outer edge of the bead seat. An additional ET number (13x6 ET 40) would indicate the offset in mm.

468.

Answer: B. Tire width (mm) / Sidewall height (percentage of width) / Wheel rim diameter (inches)

These numbers may also be shown as 205/55 R16. Additional numbers may be listed such as load rating and speed index (for example, 89V), minimum and maximum inflation PSI values, as well as DOT compliance and UTQG (Uniform Tire Quality Grade) codes.

469.

Answer: D. Both A and B

The cylinder is the cylindrical channel where the piston travels. Fuel and air are compressed and ignited in the cylinder, which contains the resulting expanding gasses. Increased pressure in the cylinder forces the piston back and transfers energy to the drive train.

470. *Automotive Information*

During the combustion stroke, expanding gasses are sealed in the cylinder by:

A. Closing the intake valve
B. Closing the exhaust valve
C. Properly fitted compression rings
D. All of the above

471. *Automotive Information*

Most cars with internal combustion engines use:

A. A rechargeable 6-volt battery
B. A lead-acid 12-volt battery
C. A rechargeable NiCad battery
D. An alternator in place of a battery

472. *Automotive Information*

The solenoid, the flywheel, and the clutch and neutral safety switches are part of:

A. The manual transmission
B. The braking system
C. The air conditioning system
D. The starter system

470.

Answer: D. All of the above

In order for the cylinder to contain the gasses created during the combustion stroke, the intake and exhaust valves must both be closed. Properly fitted compression rings prevent gas from blowing past the piston head, resulting in a loss of power.

471.

Answer: B. A lead-acid 12-volt battery

Flooded-cell batteries require periodic checking of fluid levels while sealed batteries do not require regular maintenance. Shallow cycle automotive batteries are designed to deliver a large burst of energy while starting an engine, and then be recharged by the alternator.

472.

Answer: D. The starter system

When turned on by the ignition switch, the starter motor solenoid engages the drive pinion on the starter driveshaft and turns the engine flywheel or pressure plate. In many vehicles, the transmission must be in park or neutral with the clutch in, or the brake engaged before the starter motor will operate.

473.

A starter motor is needed for most internal combustion engines because:

A. Starting without one wastes gas
B. The pistons must be in motion before the four-stroke cycle will operate smoothly
C. Starting directly using gas could damage the timing system
D. It prevents starting the engine while in gear

474.

Engine size is determined by:

A. Displacement, calculated from the mass of the engine block
B. Displacement, calculated from the cylinder bore, stroke, and number of cylinders
C. Power generation, calculated from horsepower and torque
D. Power rating, calculated from horsepower at a specific RPM

475.

Power is transmitted from the engine to the wheels in this order:

A. Drive shaft, transmission, crankshaft, axle
B. Cam shaft, transmission, drive shaft, differential, axle
C. Crankshaft, transmission, drive shaft, differential, axle
D. Engine, transmission, tie rods, axle

473.

Answer: B. The pistons must be in motion before the four-stroke cycle will operate smoothly

For the engine to engage and begin to cycle correctly, the pistons must be in motion. In early motor cars before starter motors were regularly included, the operator had to hand crank the engine before starting.

474.

Answer: B. Displacement, calculated from the cylinder bore, stroke, and number of cylinders

Displacement is a measure of how much air/fuel mixture an engine moves in one cycle. In general, the larger the displacement, the more power an engine can generate. Displacement can be measured in liters (3.4 liter) or cubic inches (312 cid).

475.

Answer: C. Crankshaft, transmission, drive shaft, differential, axle

These key components in the power train connect in sequence to transfer energy from the engine to the wheels.

476. *Automotive Information*

Pistons, crankshaft, clutch or torque converter, drive shaft, differential and axles are all part of:

A. The undercarriage
B. The power train
C. The steering system
D. The suspension system

---

477. *Automotive Information*

Which of the following components is not part of the transmission?

A. U-joint
B. Clutch
C. Torque converter
D. Transfer case

---

478. *Automotive Information*

The differential connects:

A. The torque converter and the drive shaft
B. The transmission and the axles
C. The drive shaft and the axles
D. The crankshaft and the drive shaft

476.

Answer: B. The power train

The power train encompasses the major moving parts that translate energy from fuel into movement of the vehicle.

477.

Answer: A. U-joint

The universal joint in the drive shaft allows for an offset in the alignment between the transmission and the differential. The clutch (manual), the torque converter (automatic) and transfer case (4-wheel drive) are all transmission components.

478.

Answer: C. The drive shaft and the axle

In a rear drive car, the differential transfers the rotation of the drive shaft to both rear axles. The differential allows for the variable rotation rate of the rear wheels around turns.

479.

The drive shaft connects:

A. The torque converter and the clutch plate
B. The transmission and the differential
C. The transmission and the axles
D. The crankshaft and the U-joint

480.

Which of the following instruments measures how fast the engine is turning?

A. Speedometer
B. Timing light
C. Tachometer
D. Odometer

479.

Answer: B. The transmission and the differential

The drive shaft, which may include a U-joint, connects the transmission to the differential.

480.

Answer: C. Tachometer

The tachometer measures the rate of rotation of the engine's crankshaft, expressed in revolutions per minute (RPM). There is often a red area which indicates unsafe levels. In manual transmission vehicles, the tachometer can help the driver decide the most efficient gear to be in or when to switch gears.

481. *Assembling Objects*

Select which choice represents the objects fitted together.

A   B

C   D

482. *Assembling Objects*

Select which choice represents the objects fitted together.

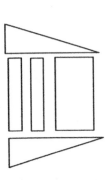 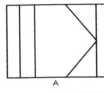 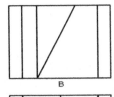

A   B

C   D

483. *Assembling Objects*

Select which choice represents the objects fitted together.

A   B

C   D

481.

Assembling Objects

Answer: A

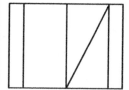

482.

Assembling Objects

Answer: C

483.

Assembling Objects

Answer: D

484. *Assembling Objects*

Select which choice represents the objects fitted together.

A

B

C

D

485. *Assembling Objects*

Select which choice represents the objects fitted together.

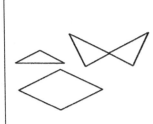

A

B

C

D

486. *Assembling Objects*

Select which choice represents the objects fitted together.

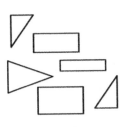

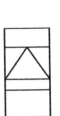
A

B

C

D

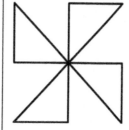

484.   *Assembling Objects*

Answer: B

485.   *Assembling Objects*

Answer: A

486.   *Assembling Objects*

Answer: A

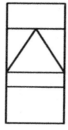

487. *Assembling Objects*

Select which choice represents the objects fitted together.

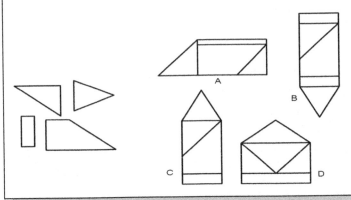

488. *Assembling Objects*

Select which choice represents the objects fitted together.

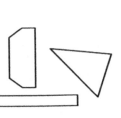

489. *Assembling Objects*

Select which choice represents the objects fitted together.

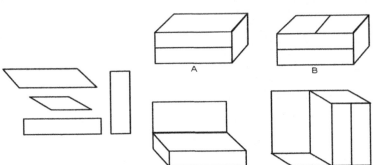

487.

Answer: C

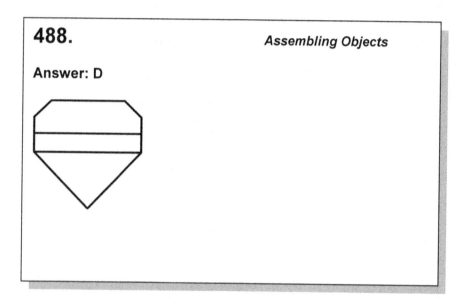

488.

Answer: D

489.

Answer: A

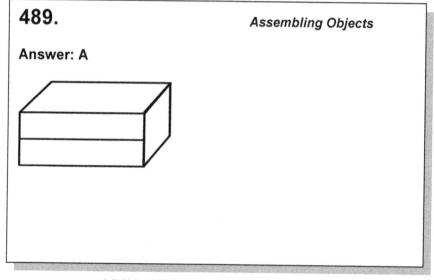

490.

Select which choice represents the objects fitted together.

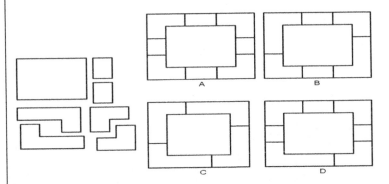

491.

Select which choice represents the two objects connected by the points indicated.

  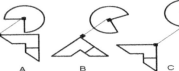

492.

Select which choice represents the two objects connected by the points indicated.

490.

Assembling Objects

Answer: B

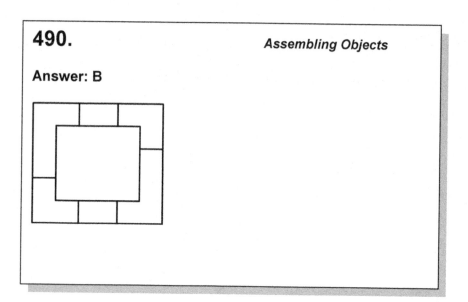

491.

Assembling Objects

Answer: B

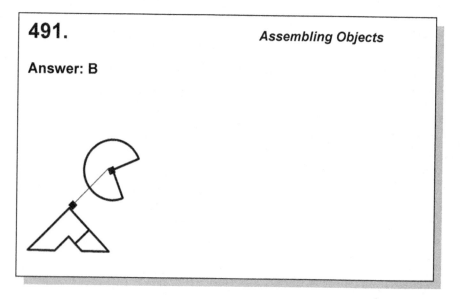

492.

Assembling Objects

Answer: C

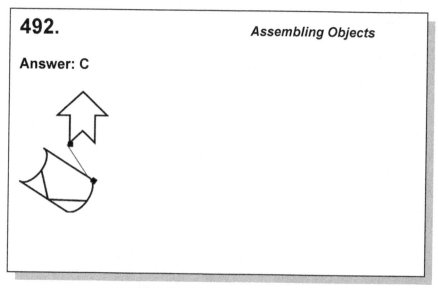

493.

Select which choice represents the two objects connected by the points indicated.

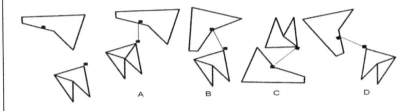

494.

Select which choice represents the two objects connected by the points indicated.

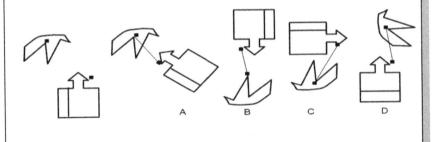

495.

Select which choice represents the two objects connected by the points indicated.

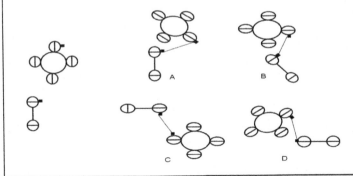

493.

Assembling Objects

Answer: D

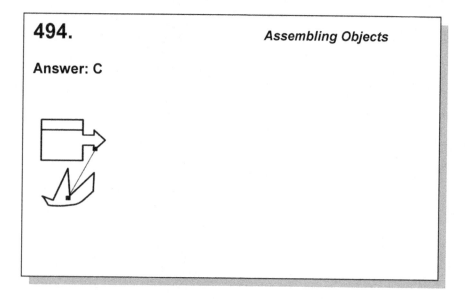

494.

Assembling Objects

Answer: C

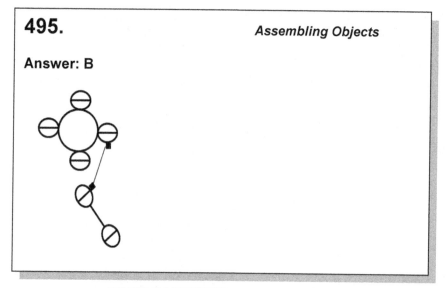

495.

Assembling Objects

Answer: B

496. *Assembling Objects*

Select which choice represents the objects fitted together.

A

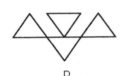
B

C

D

497. *Assembling Objects*

Select which choice represents the objects fitted together.

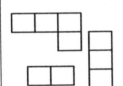

 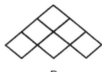
A B

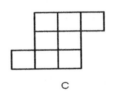
C D

498. *Assembling Objects*

Select which choice represents the two objects connected by the points indicated.

A B

C D

496.

Answer: C

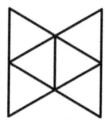

497.

Answer: A

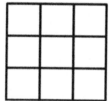

498.

Answer: D

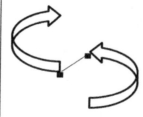

499.

Select which choice represents the two objects connected by the points indicated.

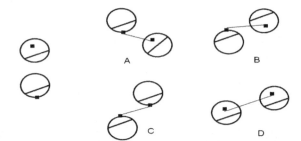

500.

Select which choice represents the two objects connected by the points indicated.

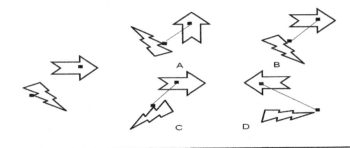

499.

Answer: B

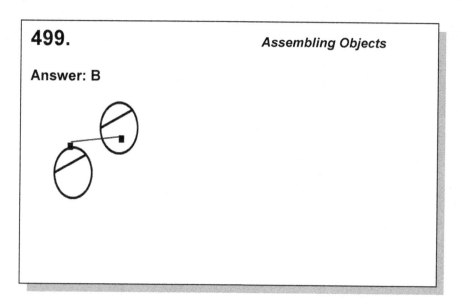

500.

Answer: A

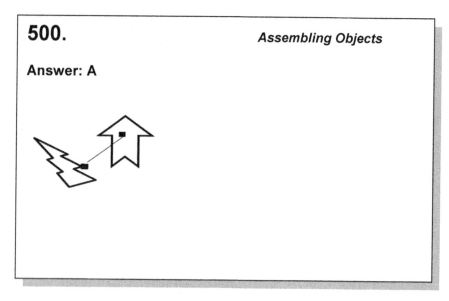

ANSWER KEY

Mathematics Knowledge/Arithmetic Reasoning

176. ---	201. D	226. D
177. ---	202. C	227. D
178. ---	203. B	228. B
179. A	204. D	229. D
180. B	205. A	230. C
181. C	206. B	231. C
182. A	207. A	232. B
183. A	208. A	233. A
184. B	209. C	234. A
185. C	210. D	235. D
186. ---	211. B	236. B
187. ---	212. B	237. D
188. A	213. C	238. D
189. C	214. A	239. C
190. D	215. C	240. A
191. B	216. B	241. C
192. A	217. D	242. C
193. B	218. A	243. A
194. A	219. C	244. B
195. C	220. C	245. A
196. B	221. A	246. C
197. B	222. B	247. D
198. D	223. D	248. B
199. A	224. D	249. B
200. B	225. A	250. A

General Science

251. C	265. C	279. D
252. B	266. B	280. A
253. A	267. D	281. C
254. A	268. C	282. A
255. A	269. C	283. A
256. B	270. D	284. C
257. A	271. A	285. A
258. B	272. D	286. C
259. C	273. C	287. B
260. B	274. C	288. C
261. C	275. C	289. A
262. C	276. D	290. A
263. A	277. B	291. D
264. D	278. C	292. C

293. C	304. A	315. B
294. A	305. B	316. A
295. A	306. A	317. A
296. B	307. C	318. B
297. C	308. C	319. D
298. A	309. B	320. B
299. C	310. C	321. C
300. A	311. A	322. B
301. A	312. C	323. A
302. D	313. B	324. C
303. A	314. B	325. C

Mechanical Comprehension

326. A	340. D	354. A
327. C	341. A	355. C
328. A	342. C	356. A
329. D	343. B	357. C
330. B	344. C	358. C
331. B	345. B	359. A
332. C	346. C	360. B
333. D	347. A	361. B
334. C	348. B	362. C
335. A	349. B	363. C
336. B	350. D	364. B
337. A	351. A	365. D
338. D	352. D	
339. A	353. A	

Electronics Information

366. B	378. D	390. B
367. C	379. B	391. C
368. D	380. D	392. A
369. A	381. B	393. B
370. C	382. A	394. D
371. A	383. C	395. A
372. D	384. D	396. D
373. B	385. C	397. B
374. A	386. A	398. C
375. C	387. C	399. B
376. B	388. D	400. C
377. A	389. A	